Otley

Past, Present and Future
25 years on

A commemoration of the life and
history of Otley

Compiled by
John Morgan

OTLEY 2002

Published by Otley P.P.F. Community Project

Compiled by John Morgan

Copyright © Otley P.P.F. Community Project Team

This book is typeset in Adobe Garamond

Designed by Creative Design Associates Limited,
Otley, West Yorkshire

Jacket photography by Winpenny Photography,
Otley, West Yorkshire

Printed and bound in Great Britain by Churchill's
Printing Company Limited, Leeds, West Yorkshire

ISBN 0-9542891-0-2

The Otley Past, Present and Future Project Team

Jo Allen
Joan Benson
Adrian Brooksbank
Elise Brumfitt
Adele Carr
Lesley Fidler
Alice Hamar
Sue Harrison

Graham Horner
Christine Hunter
David Portlock
John Morgan
Fred Wells
Christopher Winpenny
Edward Winpenny
Beverley Young

My sincere thanks to all the team for their work, particularly as a result of the short time we had available to produce this book.

Acknowledgements

Ian Andrew
Pat Anslow
Julie Asquith
Trevor Backhouse
Brian Bailey
Wendy Bannister
James Barber
Roy Barker
Ruth Blackwell
Richard Bowes
Peter Brewster
Paul Briscoe
Karen Brockbank
Joyce Calverley
David Cattanach
Carol Charnley
Mike Charnley
Hazel Costello
Eric Cowling
Ian Creswell
Les Cross
Richard Crowther
Ann Devereux

Malcolm Devereux
Brian Dexter
David Dickenson
Ron Dickenson
Ronnie Duncan
John Eveleigh
Rachel Feldburg
Crew of Otley Fire Station
Mathew Fortune
Nigel Francis
Sylvia Garthwaite
Mike Gittings
Joanna Grundy
Joanna Guise
Raoul Guise
John Harrison
Derek Hawler
Derek Hawley
Sandra Helliwell
John Holdsworth
Dave Holmwood
Margaret Hornby

Andrew Howard
Julia Johnson
Mick Kirby
Graham Kirkland
Chris Lawson
Phil Lees
Mervyn Lister
Christopher Little
Pat Lofthouse
Peter Lund
Lindsay Marsden
Neil McLellan
Carol Middleton
Lila Mitchell
Val Moore
Hilda Morgan
Fred Morrell
Meg Morton
Stella Murdoch
Rachel Nelson
Graham Newall
Colin Newton
Margaret Newton

Margaret Parkin
Owen Peel
Helen Pickersgill
Janet Raw
Penny Rhodes
Maurice Risbin
David Robson
Shirley Slater
Chris Smith
W.Clifford Smith
David Steel
Norman Stephens
Colin Swanton
Keith Urquhart
Tom Walls
Betty Watson
Alan Webster
Irene Willis
Louise Wilson
Peter Young

Photography and illustration credits:
Ian Andrew,
John Morgan,
Fred Wells,
Winpenny Photography
Paul Wood

Creative Design Associates Limited for the special help and flexibility in taking care of our printing requirements.

We hope we have covered everyone who has contributed to this book in any way – the scale and speed of the project may have led to some omissions.

Sponsors

Wm. ACKROYD (Holdings) LTD: Wharfebank Business Centre, Ilkley Road. Founded 1815. Worsted spinners until 1983. Refurbished former mill buildings now housing 55 industrial and office enterprises in spacious riverside surroundings.

ATKINSON DACRE: Solicitors, 40 Boroughgate. Have served the local business and farming communities over 125 years. Email:prwalker@Atkinson-dacre.co.uk

G.R. AUTOS: of Granville Mount. Total car and customer care. Tel.850034.

JAMES BARBER: Yorkshire's leading tobacconist. Winner of UK pipe retailer of the year 2002.

BEKS: Electrical, hardware and D.I.Y. Pleased to serve the public and thanks them for their support over the past 25 years.

BONDGATE POTTERY: Occupying two 18th Century cottages. Continues a pottery tradition in Otley. Peter and Wendy make garden, domestic and studio pots in full view of the shopper.

BROWNS GALLERY: Arguably Yorkshire's largest picture gallery is family owned and proud to offer all the major artists and a quality picture framing service.

BROWSE TIME: Courthouse Street. Books plus @ minus prices, full range of new books plus CD's, DVD's, games and vinyl's at trade discount prices.

CAROLE FASHIONS (Otley) LTD: Carole's – the fashion shop in Otley. We have been in Otley since 1947 but our clothes are 2002.

CONWAYS TOYMASTER: the largest selection of toys, games, climbing frames and outdoor toys in the area. Open 7 days a week. Tel.462065.

CRAFTSMAN TOOLS LTD: Since formation in 1953 Craftsman Tools has been at the forefront of work and toolholding technology with the skills and expertise to meet the most exacting and demanding engineering tasks.

CROSS GREEN VETERINARY CENTRE: Serving the community for over 60 years. Tel.462546.

BASIL HOULDSWORTH & SONS: Leeds Road. Joiners and builders. Training and employing local tradesmen for local contracts for over 40 years.

KINEHOLME OF OTLEY: Bradford Road. Wharfedale's longest established family owned motor dealership. Nobody knows Renault better than we do.

KORKS WINE BAR & BRASSERIE: Otley's original wine bar. Providing fine food and fine wines since 1981.

LENTOID PLASTICS LTD: Factory and shop on Gay Lane, sells direct to public. Manufacturing opticians since 1972. Ophthalmic, scientific and technical lenses for opticians and industry.

LUND OF OTLEY (Furnishings) LTD: Established in Otley over 60 years.

MAYFAIR ANTIQUES: Incorporating Frantique dealers in French and English antiques and decorative art. Owner widely published in UK and French antiques and lifestyle press.

MAYPOLE FISHERIES: Quality food with traditional values in a very popular cosy restaurant and takeaway. Sea fish quality award winners.

Sponsors

GEO. MIDDLEMISS & SON: Founded 1881 Otley market. Present shop since late 1890's. Fifth generation butchers. International competition winners Holland 2001 – turkey and ham pie and Wharfedale sausages.

MIRROR IMAGE: Mirrors, pictures, frames and framing. Friendly and professional personal service. Feature many exclusive items alongside popular local and international artwork.

PATISSERIE VIENNOISE: Confectioners and chocolatiers on Westgate.

BRIAN PICKLES: Crossgate. Established 1972. Lawnmower sales and service. Saws, shears sharpened etc. Horse clippers repaired and sharpened.

PREMIER ROLLS: Quality producers of paper rolls and computer supplies, ticketing and labelling. Customer base extends through retailers, finance, multi-national companies, central and local government and exporting.

PRODUMAX LTD: Precision engineers. Manufacturing precision components for the aircraft, telecommunications and medical industries for over 30 years.

SAFEWAY: The Manager and staff wish the town's project every success.

S.G.SCOTT: Established 1980. Working goldsmith. Diamond mounter. All items made on the premises (corner of Guycroft/Westgate).

WILLIAM SINCLAIR & SONS (Stationers) LTD: One of Otley's oldest and principal industries making stationery for world markets since 1837.

SKIPTON BUILDING SOCIETY: Offers a wide choice in financial services and a high level of customer care for the community.

STEPHEN H. SMITH: Traditional garden centre Established 1966 making it one of the first in our region. Later expanded, supplying a wide range of goods for home, garden and leisure.

TRUFFLES RESTAURANT: English & Continental cuisine served in a friendly and traditional setting. Table D'Hote and à la Carte Menus. Separate non-smoking Dining Room. Special Occasion and Party Bookings. Evenings and Sunday Lunch. Tel.01943 461861

H.J.WAYE: Traded originally as a butcher, but the company has now been established over 70 years as independent travel agents Waye & Son.

WEEGMANNS: Pork Butcher established in 1869 in present premises. Full range of locally reared pork products now including ready-made meals. Gained many awards over the years.

J.B.WILKINSON & SONS LTD: Quality traditional family butchers. Winners of many awards in the trade. Established 70 years.

WINPENNY PHOTOGRAPHY: The Studio, 3 Wesley Street. Still/Video photography. Weddings, portraits, commercial, public relations, digital services including restorations. Established 1971. Email: info@winpennyphoto.co.uk

WYKO CHEVIN: Distributors of ball and roller bearings, power transmission, pneumatics, hydraulics and much more. Call in for more details

YORKSHIRE WATER: Happy to assist.

CONTENTS

CONTENTS

Unfortunately no information was submitted relating to the following:

Athletics, Banks and Finance, The Bellman, Bethel Church, The Choral Society, Grove Hill Tennis Club,Inner Wheel, Otley Rugby Union Football Club, Rotary Chevin, Round Table, Windmill Club and the New Year Swim.

Otley has been called the 'frontier' town. This is both an apt and graphic description situated as it is at the entrance to the Yorkshire Dales. Otley is where town meets country – an industrial market town – and where diversity leads to a vigorous mix of commerce and social activity. The town had always been home to a good number of thriving businesses exhibiting a range of skills and encompassing paper production, print machinery and not so long ago chamoix leather and oatcakes together with all the activity associated with livestock farming. Otley has been fortunate in its many benefactors. My family continues to take pride in its centuries long association with the town going as far back as the foundation of Prince Henry's School and more recently the establishment of the Riverside Park area. In my father's time his gifting of the Danefield Estate to the then Urban District Council to be maintained as a well-managed afforested area for the benefit of the town and its many visitors. Strength in diversity could be claimed as the town's enduring quality, long may this continue to be the case. I wish the project every success and hope you find this book both interesting and informative.

G N Le G Horton-Fawkes

A MESSAGE FROM THE TOWN MAYOR

I welcome the opportunity of endorsing John Morgan's updated edition of *Otley, Past, Present and Future*. The new book has been much expanded with many new features.

This book will be a must for all those people who live in and care about Otley. Many thanks to all those who have made contributions to this book. To quote from the preface of the 1977 book – "A book about the community by the community"

Councillor Gerard Francis Town Mayor of Otley
May 2002.

Preface

This book has been produced for two reasons: to provide an updated and expanded resource for Otley and to raise money for community projects. The format has been kept essentially the same as the 1977 book because this was so successful, not just in Otley, but with schools in Yorkshire, and people abroad.

Headed by myself as project co-ordinator, our team worked very well, and very hard, to bring this book to the community. Five members of the team, on behalf of the whole group, applied for, and were given Millennium Award Grants. The team enlisted the help of over one hundred people from the community and it has been a wonderful opportunity to bring people together and achieve something really worthwhile.

We used modern technology to achieve our aims, which was a mixed blessing, giving some advantages and some disadvantages. The preparation of this book would make an interesting story in its own right. The time scale for production was short, as we only secured a guarantee of funding on 23 January 2002. The pace of work necessary to get the book completed in time for the Jubilee celebrations may have given rise to some errors or omissions, which we deeply regret.

The change in society has been marked: information from public services and banks has not been forthcoming so readily as in 1977 due to centralisation and privatisation. This meant that archives have not been maintained and remote decision making has left little sympathy for, and understanding of, local communities. For this reason, banking and finance does not appear in this edition and we are very sorry for those who supported this venture but are not included. For those of you who may have been missed out, or feel that there is more to say, we can only apologise and offer the opportunity to redress any omissions through inclusion in the Otley Audio Archive project. Anyone needing to get in touch with a local club or organisation, should contact the Community Development Officer of the Council. For those of you who have further interest in our local history, we can do no better than direct you to our local museum.

Our grateful thanks go to the Millennium Commission who provided our major grant. We also thank the CIT who gave us a grant, and Otley Town Council who organised a guaranteed loan to cover printing costs. Our sponsors gave willingly and generously and we are pleased to record them in this book. Most importantly, we thank those who purchase the book because all proceeds go directly to Otley community ventures and one of the major beneficiaries will be the Maypole project. Sales of the book will multiply the original Millennium Commission Grant. I am very pleased to take this opportunity to express my sincere thanks to my team. All of their skills and abilities were essential to the finished product. Thanks also to the very great number of people who provided information. Between us all, a better understanding exists and friendships have been made.

John Morgan May 2002

Jubilee Celebrations 1977

The Jubilee Committee presented numerous events which included the publishing of the original *Otley Past, Present & Future* book, a simple river festival, a dance at the Civic Centre with a monster tombola (thanks to local shops), and the Chevin Beacon. All these events helped raise funds for the Meals on Wheels Kitchen, which still serves the

town. A pig roast took place in Manor Square but that was not for meals on wheels, just a BBQ on wheels. Numerous street parties took place around the town. A sponsored walk up the Washburn Valley was enjoyed by a large group of Otley folk.

Jubilee Projects 2002

The Jubilee Committee of Otley Town Council advertised for suggestions from local people for projects that would be suitable to celebrate the Jubilee in Otley, as well as life in the town. *Otley, Past, Present and Future*, a book produced at the time of the 1977 Jubilee, was chosen as that project with a greatly revised, up to date edition to be published.

On the 23 January, the Council offered the OPPF Team a loan to cover printing costs so work could start in earnest. The team put in many long hours to meet the short deadline in the hope that the book would be available in time for the Jubilee.

Local Government

Our local government officers and councillors have a thousand years of tradition and earlier reorganisation from which to draw their expertise. Medieval towns such as Otley developed almost entirely on the strength of their markets and continue to this day to maintain strong rural links. The present strength of local government is better understood by a knowledge of its development from its rudimentary form in the middle-ages.

Shire Courts and Sheriff: When the famous William conquered England in 1066 he took on the English institutions known as the Shire Courts, with their officers, the Sheriffs. The Sheriff held extensive authority and he presided over the County Court. Each County was divided into 'hundreds' with its own court and Bailiff.

Domesday: In the late eleventh century, William compiled the report known as the Domesday Book, to settle once and for all, many disputes about land. Domesday established the Manor with the whole of its territory under the lord's rule. The court became the Manorial Court. It is interesting to note that when Domesday was compiled there were around 1,500 'tenants' holding land from the King, 180 of whom received an annual income of £100. Of these 'tenants' only two were English.

Boroughs: The smallest area of the medieval system of local government was the vile or township and with the growth of trade in the mid twelfth century the English Borough was created, bringing with it a new civic consciousness. Tradesmen and merchants began to organise themselves and later the Boroughs were granted Royal Charters, creating a uniform move towards self-government. The possession of such a Royal Charter made a town into a Borough and this assumed great importance when Boroughs became Parliamentary Constituencies.

Magna Carta: When King John placed the Royal Seal on this document in 1215, the foundation stone of English liberty and self-government was laid. Although Magna Carta itself was a hotchpotch of baronial grievances, here and there in the mixture appeared the famous clauses which benefited classes other than just the Barons. This legal document was the guide to the development of the modern British Constitution and formed the first break with the monarchy which set us on the right path towards modern local government.

Parish Government: During the seventeenth and eighteenth centuries local government was chiefly parochial, and concerned with the relief of destitution. Members of the Parish were appointed to such unpopular and unpaid jobs as surveyor of highways, parish constable and overseers of the poor. The local government body to whom they were accountable was the 'gentry' consisting usually of the squire, the clergyman, the innkeeper and a few farmers.

Industrial Revolution: The Industrial Revolution brought about such a rapid growth in population that the rural system of local government became totally inadequate to deal with the increase in refuse, sewage, disease, river pollution and crime. Turnpike Trusts were established in an attempt to deal with the road improvement programme and finally the Parliamentary Reform Act of 1832 transferred the government of Britain from the landed aristocracy to the middle classes.

Reform of Local Government and the Otley Board: The reform of local government was finally brought about by the Poor Law Amendment Act, 1834 and the Municipal Corporations Act, 1835, which reorganised the Boroughs. Many local government Acts were to follow. By adoption of the Local Government Act, 1858, the Otley Local Board was constituted in 1864 and met in a house at 54 Kirkgate. Unfortunately, by 1885, the structure of local government was aptly described as 'chaotic': administrative confusion was remedied by the Local Government Act of 1888 which created County Borough Councils and County Council. The Local Government Act of 1884 created Urban and Rural District Councils, Parish Councils and Parish Meetings and it was in 1894 that the Otley Local Board became Otley UDC and Council Offices were purchased in North Parade. Local Government was further reorganised by an Act in 1933.

The Local Government Act of 1972, taking effect in 1974, reshaped local government on radical lines, redistributing all functions of local authorities. With this Act, attendance allowances and expenses were introduced for both County and City Councillors. Town and Parish Councillors continued as voluntary occupations.

In 1974, Otley Town Council as a Parish within Leeds Metropolitan District moved its meetings to the former Rural District Council chamber on Boroughgate and the North Parade buildings were sold. In 1986 the West Yorkshire Council was disbanded and its responsibilities assumed by the City Council and joint boards. The closure of the council chamber in Boroughgate in 1981 meant that meetings of Otley Town Council moved to the Civic Centre.

Otley Town (Parish Council) comprises 15 ward councillors representing five wards. It has an annually elected Mayor and raises a local rate precept. In 2002, Otley has the highest local rate precept in the whole Leeds area. The Otley and Wharfedale ward of Leeds City Council is served by three councillors, covering Pool, Arthington, Carlton, Bramhope and parts of Yeadon and Rawdon. These three councillors lead the Community Involvement Teams.

Otley Armed Association

The Museum of Otley possesses two important documents connected with the history of the town, both dating from 1798, when England was under threat of invasion by Napoleon. One concerns the formation of the 'Otley Armed Association', which gave the 180 names of local men who agreed to enrol themselves for the purpose of forming an Armed Association for the protection of the township of Otley and the 12 neighbouring townships, but stressed they 'will not be subject or liable to be marched out of the township of Otley or district'. The other document is the Charter authorising the Association to bear a coat of arms.

The Rev. James Bailey, vicar of Otley, on behalf of the Association, applied for a grant of arms with allusion to the Liberty of Cawood, Wistow and Otley, by which united denominations the Liberty of Otley under the Archbishops of York has always been distinguished. These arms were granted on 5th October 1798, and are unique in that they were granted to an un-corporated body.

On the formation of Otley Urban Council in 1894, they appropriated those arms as the 'arms of Otley', which was incorrect as they were not entitled to do so, and it was not until 1951 that the Council procured their own coat of arms, which they based on the original.

Civic Regalia

Otley Parish Church was the scene of a special service and ceremony on 18th May 1952, when the badge and chain of office to be worn by the Chairman of Otley Urban District Council, and the Coat of Arms which had been granted to the town, were dedicated. The cost of the regalia, £300, was fully met by public subscription. The appeal was launched by Councillor H T Spence and it was fitting that the day before he completed his two years as Chairman of the Council, he should be the first to be invested with the chain of office. The Council also made history by obtaining the Patent of Arms for the township at a

Opposite page: Kirkgate down the ages. Top: 1920's. Middle: When? Bottom: 2002

cost of one hundred guineas, 'to be borne and used for ever hereafter by the Otley Urban District Council and by its successors'.

To mark Coronation year, another badge of office to be worn by the Chairman's Lady, was also presented to the Council by the townswomen of Otley. The badge can be worn as either a pendant or brooch; it is of the finest materials and craftsmanship; of eighteen carat gold and is white and green. The centre bears the Otley Coat of Arms in enamel surrounded by white gold. The outer rim is natural gold in Chippendale style and bears three Yorkshire Roses representing the three Ridings. In 1966, a third badge of office, also purchased by public subscription, was presented to the Council, to be worn by the Vice-Chairman. The badge has a gold base and surround, with the centre composed of the Otley Coat of Arms in blue and white enamel.

After local Government re-organisation in 1974, the lettering on each badge of office was altered to read 'Town Mayor of Otley', 'Mayoress of Otley' and 'Deputy Mayor of Otley' respectively.

Lord Mayor of Leeds

Dr Graham Kirkland appointed Lord Mayor of Leeds for the year 1998/9 having served Otley on Leeds City Council for 24 years.

Honorary Citizens

An honour inaugurated in 1977 and bestowed upon local people in recognition of their services to the community. Nominations can come from anybody in the community and the honour is granted by the decision of Otley Town Council. A scroll of names is in the foyer of the Civic Centre.

Jack Simpson Awards

Two annual awards are made by Otley Sports Council. One is an award for Service to Sport to recognise someone who has served sport in Otley over the years. The second is an award for achievements in sport to an Otley person who has achieved a high degree of proficiency in a sport, or has overcome physical difficulty to attain success amongst their peers.

Community Involvement Teams

In an attempt to devolve some power from the centre of the Leeds District Council, area teams have been set up. The team for the Otley area comprises three Leeds City Council Ward Councillors plus representatives from the community with an annual budget to be used on local projects within specific guidelines. Local people can apply directly to them for grants towards projects.

Community Transport

A registered Charity (1048341) to which over 30 groups are affiliated. Formed during the 1970s to provide cost price transport to voluntary groups. The transport relieves the social isolation of elderly people by transporting them to events. It also takes local schools on field trips and sporting groups to competitions. A new vehicle was purchased at Christmas 2001.

Town Partnership

A Forum comprising of Leeds City Council, Otley Town Council, Community Groups and the Chamber of Trade. It will probably administer the Market Towns Initiative Fund, aimed at rejuvenating such towns as Otley.

Community Development Committee

A policy making committee of Otley Town Council that has co-opted members from the community present at its meetings. It is the main grant making committee of the Council.

Local Advisory Sports Council

Set up in 1972 by the Sports Council of GB (now Sports England). Main aims and objectives are to promote sports and its benefits, to campaign for better sporting facilities and safeguard those existing, and to be an advice centre for local sports clubs. They are independent of the local authority but work in close association with the statutory bodies. Their membership is open to any local sports club.

Community Council

It was the desire of the many voluntary and statutory groups to work together that initiated the Otley Community Council in 1973. It was established to promote any charitable purposes for the benefit of Otley, in particular the advancement of education, the furtherance of health and the relief of poverty, distress and sickness. It strives to promote co-operation between statutory authorities and voluntary organizations.

Any organization is eligible to be a member of the Otley Community Council by virtue of its work in the town. There are no financial ties unless that organisation considers it to be advantageous to help with some major project. In 1983 the Community Council became a Registered Charity. In the 1990s two major sub-groups, The Otley Community Transport and the Talking Newspaper, became independent charities in their own right.

The Community Council has initiated and been involved in many projects in the town over the years and now acts as a central source of information about organisations and services in the town. Because of its position as a registered charity, it is able to support relevant groups wishing to get started, help with administrative costs and fulfil its role as an umbrella organisation if required.

Britain in Bloom

During 1986, Otley began to take this competition seriously when David Smith, employed by 'Keep Britain Tidy', brought his enthusiasm and ideas to the Town

Council. A year after being last in the category 'Larger Small Towns' Otley won the coveted 'Most Improved' Rose Bowl trophy by being placed second and in 1988, won the Winners Shield. Amongst other floral displays there were over 100 hanging baskets in town centre and Otley was declared litter free. The competition brings together the Town Council, Chamber of Trade, staff of Parks and Cleansing Departments, Wharfedale General Hospital, schools, pubs, local businesses and householders. Judging takes place in spring and summer and presentations to the winners made during August.

Citizens Advice Bureau

Aims to ensure that individuals do not suffer through ignorance of their rights and responsibilities, or of the services available. The organisation also seeks to exercise responsible influence on local and national social policies.

The Citizens Advice Bureau is independent, impartial and confidential.

Situated in Courthouse Street, it is funded by Leeds City Council and surrounding Parish Councils. The grant by Otley Town Council is the largest grant made from its rate precept.

Library and Tourist Information

The Library also houses the tourist information facility as well as the IT facility which will soon have Internet access available. There is also a Local Events notice board and the facility for organisations to mount window displays. The Story Telling Group is proving very popular.

Otley Twinning Association

Otley became formally twinned with Montereau in 1980. Prior to that exchanges had taken place between students of Prince Henry's Grammar School, Otley Rotary Club and Otliensians Rugby Club. Montereau is in France, 73km southeast of Paris, situated at the confluence of the rivers Seine and Yonne. The Association is a non-political self-funding organisation, whose aim is to promote contacts and understanding between Otley and similar communities outside the U.K. Anyone can be a member provided they are prepared to reciprocate hospitality to French guests in their own homes when they visit Otley on official exchanges.

The Evolving Town

Geology

Three hundred million years ago, where Otley now stands was five degrees south of the equator in the middle of a continent called Laurasia and a great river delta covered northern England. This delta would be flooded by the sea, which left widespread layers of fossil-bearing muds. After many million years the whole delta was buried deeply under swamps which flourished in the tropical environment. Eventually, ripples from

1874: Where is this?

great earth movements in southern Britain and northern Europe, fractured and folded these Carboniferous rocks to lay the foundations of our present landscape. The south-

ward dipping rocks of Otley Chevin form an escarpment on which ancient deltaic sands have hardened into the rough grits, which have provided so much sturdy building material for the neighbourhood. Some of the grits, broken by weathering into massive blocks are tumbled over the hillside at Caley Crags and elsewhere. On their weathered surfaces are patterns of lines marking successive sandbeds deposited at flood time by an ancient fast flowing river.

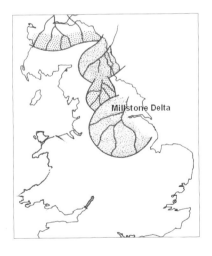

Laurasia drifted slowly northwest on a giant raft some hundred miles thick. Continental and marine conditions alternated, leaving their mark in East Yorkshire, though not in Otley. 150 million years ago Laurasia split from North America and Greenland. Near the western edge of Eurasia, the Pennine chain began to rise some 50 million years ago at the beginning of the Tertiary era. River valleys formed on its eastern flank, the beginning of the eastward flowing pattern of the Yorkshire Dales. During the Tertiary era, the world's climate became cooler. Eventually, about three million years ago, the area reached its present latitude and the arctic ice cap began to grow, moulding the landscape with enormous erosive power as it advanced and retreated. Following its last retreat, about eleven thousand years ago, it left patches of stony boulder clay whose properties are only too well known to local gardeners. For a while a glacier flowed down Wharfedale, ending somewhere near Pool where its terminal moraine can be detected by the trained eye. This must have played a substantial part in shaping the broad Wharfedale valley that we know. Finally, it too retreated, its melt waters leaving important deposits of coarse gravel.

Prior to the Ice Age, the Wharfe was a small river starting somewhere east of Otley. This small but vigorous stream cut back westwards though its bed of soft shales, meeting a tributary of the Aire flowing from the northwest through the 'Guiseley gap' between Otley Chevin and the Baildon Moor. The long tributary of the Aire was quickly captured by its small companion and its flow diverted eastwards, becoming the upper Wharfe and cutting a broad valley in the shale north of Addingham Edge and Otley Chevin.

Over millions of years, the Wharfe has meandered along its floodplain, sometimes depositing sand and gravels, sometimes cutting down a few feet to a lower level leaving 'river terraces'. Portions of the earlier floodplain include that on which Ashfield House now stands, and the one up which Burley Road climbs just before joining the main road from Menston to Ilkley.

During the last retreat of the glaciers, the Wharfe in spate must have been a powerful erosive agent. Where it was checked in its course and deflected eastwards by the mass of the Chevin, it deposited its load of valuable river gravels west of Otley. It also attacked the obstacles in its path, easily undercutting the shales at the base of the Chevin. After heavy rain the over-steepened shale slopes no longer supported the overlying sandstones and masses of the cliff slid down and spread halfway across the valley, forcing the river into a more northerly channel almost up against the sandstone of Billams Hill. Looking across from Blubberhouses road, the characteristic hummocky surface of the old landslips can be seen; the most notable being the wooded scar of the Great Dib.

This last scene of our geological drama sets the stage for human occupation; the lower slopes of the landslips lie above flood level yet closer to the river in its restricted floodplain and sheltered by the Chevin from south-westerly storms. Perhaps we can see here an ideal resting place for the first hunters and fishers to explore the district.

Mesolithic (11,000 – 3,500 BC)

Some thirteen thousand years ago, the ice of the Glacial Period had retreated northward from Mid-Wharfedale and left a bare landscape of hillsides with stunted woods and valleys full of lakes and swamps. To the east and west of where the bridge over the Wharfe now stands, were large lakes, and it is on the banks of these lakes we find the traces of the coming of Mesolithic peoples, the last of the old Stone Age hunters, who made the link with Neolithic man.

Fallen blocks on the Chevin.

They were a small people, the men no more than 5' 4" tall, and the women correspondingly less. They were hunters, food gatherers, and wild fowlers, who had shelters of hides and used the same material for clothing. Their tools were of imported flint – scraper, gravers, borers, saws, knives and eventually axes. With these they made bows and arrows, spears, fish spears and wooden hafts. They had dogs and used them for hunting.

We know from the small camping sites on the hills that they followed the annual spring and autumn migrations of the large game to spring pastures. They appear to have had birch canoes and dugout boats and doubtless made fishing nets. During their long occupations of the North of England, they developed some of the domestic arts, which we enjoy today. By storing meat in guts they invented the sausage. By treating the inner bark of the birch with heat they made a waterproof glue. They dried and rolled birch bark in a strip and stood the roll on one end, applied a light and had the first candles. Their finest achievement was the making of the first hafted stone axe to cope with the increasing forest growth

They hunted roe and red deer, the auroch, elk and pig, and were capable of dealing with bears. Sometime in the ninth millennium BC, they appear to have deserted the lakeside settlements and we find the tools of later peoples on the hill ridges.

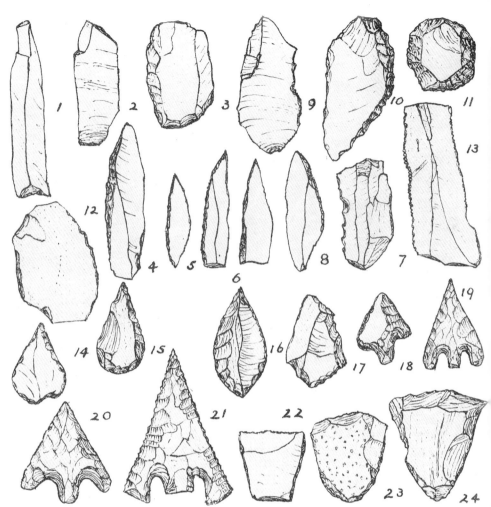

1. *Graver*   2. *Grave*   3. *Scraper*   4. *Borer*   5. *Bird Throttle*   6. *Two Harpoon Barbs*   7. *Saw (Early Mesolithic - Terrace Site, Otley)*   8. *Harpoon Barb (Late Mesolithic - Rombalds Moor)*   9. *Graver* 10. *Side Scraper*   11. *Thumb Scraper (Late Mesolithic - Terrace Site, Otley)*   12. *Knife (Neolithic - Terrace Site, Otley)*   13. *Saw (Bronze Age - Green Crag Slack)*   14. *Pear Shaped Point (Neolithic - Green Crag Slack)*   15. *Pear Shaped Point (Neolithic - Askwith Moor)*   16. *Leaf Shaped Point (Neolithic - Green Crag Slack)*   17. *Kite Shaped Point (Neolithic - Green Crag Slack)*   18. *Tanged Point (Neolithic - Otley)*   19. *Barbed And Tanged Point (Bronze Age - Langshaw Beck)*   20. *Barbed And Tanged Point*   21. *Amoucan Point (Bronze Age - Green Crag Slack)*   22. *Transverse Arrowpoint (Mesolithic - Weston Moor)*   23. *Transverse Arrowpoint (Neolithic - Green Bank)*   24. *Transverse Arrowpoint (Bronze Age - Askwith Moor)*   Drawings are actual size.*

Neolithic (3,500 – 2,500 BC)

During this period gravel was extracted from the hummocky ground between the River Wharfe and Newall.

In 1970, workmen found bones in soil which gave a date about 3,000 BC. These went to the Otley Museum for examination. The remains included the bones of a female, a dog, two kinds of cow, a pig and a horse. Scattered amongst the remains were many hazel nuts, a main food for early man. Historically, this is an important find as it records the beginnings of pastoral Wharfedale some 5,000 years ago.

Romano-British

By the time of the coming of Christ, the Brigantes in this part of the world had settled down to a life of mixed farming. This appears to have continued until they were taken over by the Angles in the seventh century. They were principally raisers of cattle but sheep must have been reared for they will feed where cattle cannot. Pigs were kept and fed in the surrounding woods. We know by the discovery of querns, or hand cornmills, that they grew cereals and the varying types of querns prove that the occupation of Otley was continuous.

Their dwellings were circular huts with stone walls and roofs of heather. Two or three huts were often enclosed by a wall and there were many stone built pounds for the protection of stock. Their cereals were grown in small square field, preferably on a slope. There would be a kiln for the drying of grain and sometimes a circular enclosure of standing stones for religious and civic meetings. The ways of the Romans were imposed on the Britons. In Agricola's days all local villages would provide gangs for road making. The quarries they made are still to be seen on the Chevin and the stones of the road were re-used to build the present day field walls.

Throughout the Roman occupation the Roman army would require local levies of manpower and tribute would be paid in produce of the settlement. Proof that the local Britons adopted Roman ways is found in the domestic altar which came from the walls of the church and which must have adorned the doorway of some local Briton of importance.

Burials are reported from the church yard where the corpse was laid out in a pit along with flint tools and a roof of tiles erected above. Such burials are found in York and would be pagan burials. When the chancel of the church had the floor lowered, a stone lined grave was found which only contained a knot of human hair. This might well be the burial place of a British saint. Many of the stone coffins found at York are said to be of Otley stone and the same material was used for the querns found in the district. The nearness of the Roman fort at Ilkley, the Roman capital at York and the road connecting the two must have brought much Roman influence to Otley. Many local inhabitants must have taken up employment at York and other Roman stations.

Anglians (410-937 AD)

It is to the Angles and their followers, the Vikings, that we owe the main features of our cultural heritage. They gave us our languages, the basis of our legal system, the spread of Christianity, our system of farming and most of our surnames and place names.

The Angles first came to York as early as the fifth century as missionaries and during the following 200 years they spread over England during a series of wars between Britons and Angles and rival Anglia chieftains. In 660 AD, Oswy, King of Northumbria, defeated and slew Penda, King of Mercia, who led a mixed army of Mercians and Britons. Some three years later Oswy called a synod of churchmen at Whitby and it was there decided that the whole kingdom should follow the practices of the Church of Rome. The peace caused by this union lead to the building of many churches and Christian crosses. One of the earliest of these crosses was the Angel Cross at Otley, pieces of which are in the Parish Church and Museum at Otley with a replica in the Memorial Park at Otley. This cross is dated between 675 and 750 AD and is proof of a strong Christian community at that time. The arm of a smaller cross, now in the Museum, shows a Viking warrior fully arrayed in armour with spear, sword, dagger, shield and helmet. This man monument records the head man in Otley about 900-950 AD.

The name of Otley itself is interesting. In early records the name is Ottanlege. Ottan probably stands for the personal name 'Otta', referring to an Anglian chief who was a strong swimmer. 'Lege' is another form of 'ley' meaning an open space or clearing. Thus the name Otley records the name of the first Otleyite.

In 937, Athelstan, King of England, met and defeated a mixed army of Scottish and Irish Vikings at the Battle of Brunanberg in Scotland. As a reward for the Archbishop of York's services, Athelstan presented him with the Liberty of Otley. This large estate was centred on Otley with a wooden hall on what is now the site of the Manor House. Since that time, Otley has been the administrative and legal centre and it is probable that it was already a market town.

The Parish Church of All Saints

The date and foundation of the Parish Church of All Saints is not known. There is little documentary evidence about any pre-Conquest church, but it is not unlikely the first church at Otley was built in the eighth or ninth century, and substantial surviving fragments of Anglo-Saxon crosses are evidence of this. These were preaching crosses, and pre-date the erection of a church. Of the three principal ones, on a pedestal in the Baptistry, one has busts of the Evangelists and is a unique piece of sculpture, known as the 'Angel' cross and dated 750 A.D. Another depicts two eagles with dragon's tails, the details being clear cut and full of symbolic significance. This is the 'Dragon' cross, of date 800 A.D. A third is of completely different style with scrolls and strapwork, which is dated 860 A.D.

The first Norman church of the twelfth century, was built on the foundations of the Saxon structure, and is now the Chancel, which retains the Norman Piscina, aumbry and two small windows high up in the walls. In 1240 AD, the Church was enlarged by the addition of the Nave, Transepts and Tower and between 1485-1500 the two aisles were completed and the large East window inserted. In 1851 the present roof and clerestory were added to the Nave and in 1867 further restoration included the removal of the two galleries which had been put up in the previous century, and the replacement of the old 'box' pews by the present oak seats.

The Tower contains eight bells, which were last re-cast in 1922. The church clock, made

Otley Parish Church.

F. Morrell..........1976.

by Harrison of Aberford, dates from 1793, at which time the unusual carillon was added. These played a different tune each day of the week but have not been heard in recent years.

Notable monuments in the church include a brass dated 1593 recording the alliances of the Palmes of Ripon and the Lindleys of Lindley: the tomb of the first Lord and Lady Fairfax of Denton and the tombs of Dyneley of Bramhope, Vavasour of Stead, Fawkes, Barker, and Lacon amongst others.

The Registers were commenced in 1562 and contain many interesting entries, which include the signature of John Wesley as officiant at a wedding in 1788 and also the baptism of Thomas Chippendale in 1718. The church possesses a book of sermons preached in this and other churches by Dissenting Ministers during the Civil War. This is handwritten by Charles Fairfax of Menston in a code known only to him and has yet not been decoded.

In the churchyard is a monument in memory of all the men who lost their lives in the construction of Bramhope Tunnel, between 1845-49. The unusual style represents in minature the entrance of the tunnel at Arthington.

A brass plate in church lists our vicars from 1627. The church is not a museum, but a living institution and remains, since its foundation as an active centre of life.

In the new Millennium there is something for everyone at the Parish Church: from the choir to the Mothers' Union, started one hundred and ten years ago by Mrs Horton Fawkes; the Newall Ladies' Fellowship; the Men's Fellowship group which meets in the Parish Room; brownies, guides, beavers, cubs, scouts and the Friendship Club for older people.

Hopefully, today's Parish Registers will make interesting reading for future generations. They will record such events as: the marriage of Mark James, the golfer, to Jane in 1980, the appointment of our first female churchwarden Shirley Parker and the construction of the Parish Room at the rear of the church during 1990/1. Situated in the former Baptistry, this required special permission to move the font to its current position at the front of the church and the building of five town houses in 1995 in what was formerly the Church Schoolroom.

Otley All Saints Bellringers

Otley Parish Church has a ring of eight bells, forming an octave in the key of F. Originally hung in the mid-18th century, they were recast in 1922. The tenor (heaviest) bell weighs just over 16 cwt, the treble (lightest) about 4 cwt. During the Foot and Mouth outbreak of 2001 the bells were rung at 11am each Monday morning when the Auction Mart should have been starting its day's business, signifying our support for the farming community, and a peal of bells rang out when the first market was held again in 2002.

A brass plate in church lists our vicars from 1267, starting with Galfridus de Bridlington and finishing with that of Graham Buttanshaw, our current vicar who came to Otley after working in Sudan and Uganda. He is ably assisted by our curate, Philip Moon, and together they are helping us anticipate the future of Christianity in Otley with excitement.

The Archbishop's Palace

In 1968 a local history class undertook a 'dig' supervised by J Le Patourel, prior to the building of St Joseph's School on the site. The object was to investigate the remains of the Manor house first mentioned in 1226 with reference to Archbishop Gray who granted a fair and market, founded a borough and gave encouragement to the building of a bridge. In a survey of 1307, the Otley house has a very high value compared with the other 11 in Yorkshire. Ten years later the town and house were badly damaged by Scots raiders for which the Scots were excommunicated by Melton.

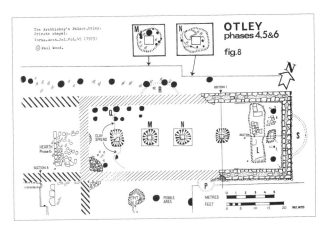

The dig uncovered a free-standing apsidal stone built chapel, which succeeded timber buildings, and is of Saxon or Norman date. This had been incorporated later into a range of buildings with an upper floor chapel and private apartments. A well made covered drain ran under the west end of the block. In the thirteenth century the chapel was again altered and extended by the addition of a square end instead of the apse, and more buildings to the west.

The scalloped capital, now in the Museum, was found being re-used as a stylobate and was dated about 1150.

There was little pottery: only ten shards were dated from c650-c850. There were five Saxo-Norman rims and the rest up to the end of the eighteenth century.

Other finds included animal bones, an almost complete skeleton of a very large dog or wolf, a socketed arrowhead, (probably thirteenth century) and coins, the earliest a King John penny c1205-10, also a Robert II of Scotland penny 1371-1390.

The present Manor House was built in 1792 and there is a comprehensive literature on the Archbishop's Palace in Otley Museum.

Historical Stepping Stones

AD 937 The Granting of The Liberty: Archbishop Walstan of York helped the ruling Saxon King Athelstan scatter gathering Viking forces in Lowland Scotland. For this service, the Archbishop was granted an estate known as 'The Liberty of Otley, Cawood and Wistow'. It was shrewd gift, the strategic position of Otley effectively cut off the best potential invasion route up the Ribble and down the Wharfe to York for the many beaten Vikings who had fled to Ireland.

AD 1100 Henry I: The King made a brave and mainly successful attempt to unite the nation and in a bid to make his position as a usurper secure, he granted 'The Charter of Liberties'. One of his promises in this was to abolish feudal laws and restore the laws of Edward the Confessor.

AD 1130 Building the Mill Dam: According to records there was a mill in Otley in 1130. Water was the only source of power so the building of the mill dam, a major construction task, must have been completed then.

AD 1222 Granting of a Charter for a Market and a Fair: Otley was one of the first towns to be granted a charter. Henry III, although only an infant, granted a market charter to Walter Gray, Archbishop of York, for his town of Otley. (NB: A book complied by Messrs E Cowling and F Morrell from early manuscripts depicts life Otley during this period of history in much detail.)

AD 1419 Refusal by the Royal Foresters to pay Market Toll: Royal Foresters, by ancient right, were exempt from toll when attending a market. When an attempt to override this privilege was made, 7,000 men of the forest arrived on Otley Bridge. The men of Otley offered no resistance and the 'outrage' passed over without bloodshed.

AD1611 Founding of Prince Henry's Grammar School: See the article on 'Education'.

AD1718 Chippendale of Otley: With the spread of culture, there came at this period a demand for fine furniture and fittings to fill the many grand houses which were springing up. Of the craftsmen, none is more famous than Thomas Chippendale.

AD 1841 Turnpike Road between Otley and Leeds: During the eighteenth and nineteenth centuries, increasing population and trade called for new means of transport. Packhorse tracks gave way to roads because four horses on a metalled road could pull a load equal to that carried by forty pack ponies. The Old Road to Leeds was steep and slow and a new turnpike road, the New Leeds Road, took its place in 1841.

AD 1857 The Birth of the Wharfedale Printing Machine: Otley people must be very proud that the idea of a mechanical printing press was largely due to a few mid nineteenth century Otley men and without doubt, the perfecting of the machine was almost wholly their work. William Dawson and his apprentice David Payne, pioneered not only a great boon to industry in the town but to knowledge and learning throughout the civilised world.

Otley Bridge

1228: The Archbishop's records give us the first reference to the bridge. Originally five spans of ribbed arches.

1538: Richard Langfellay left 40 shillings for repairs to the bridge.

1623: Considerable storm damage left the bridge in need of repairs amounting to £250.

1673: The bridge was destroyed by a great flood.

1775: The old structure was retained while the bridge was widened on the upstream side parapets were rebuilt, two arches added, and a footwalk of flagstones was provided at a cost of £750.

1957: The cantilevered footwalk was added, flag stones were removed, the roadway widened, the surface tarred, traffic lights removed and two-way traffic allowed. It is today the only remaining medieval bridge over the river Wharfe. It has been classed as an ancient monument.

Place Names

This selection on local place names was complied by children from St Joseph's school and is based upon Extent of Otley 1307.

Otley 947 AD taken from Chevin

    1130 AD Ottenlage

    1195 AD Otelai

Chevin: The Chevin is the well-known hill overlooking Otley, it is mentioned in 972 as *Scefing* and in the York Gospel Book as Acefinge. Ekwall suggests that the initial 'S' in *Scefing* is the remains of an original IS meaning 'below'. *Scefing* being the Welsh Cefn or the 'place below the ridge', *Scefing* would then be the early name for Otley. This supposition is supported by the fact that the slope of the hill is named Chevin Moor. All the common pastures on the slopes above the neighbouring villages were 'moors' and we have Burley Moor, Denton Moor, and so on. If Chevin Moor got the name from the town then the town must have been named *Scefing*.

Otley: The first written record of Otley was in the York Gospel Book of 1030 as *Ottenlege*, in the Domesday Book it was *Otleia* and in the Pipe Rolls of 1195 we have *Ottelia*. Ley is one of the common-est terminations and is from the *OE leah*, 'a clearing', either natural or made, usually in a wooded area. *Otta* was most likely a personal name of *OE* usage and used as a byname, coming from oter, 'the otter'. This, the first recorded citizen of Otley, must have been a very good swimmer.

Wharfe *OS*: Ekwall says a British river name meaning a wading stream and derived form
OE warpen 'to throw' Latin verbana. From this Roman Verbeia upon Roman inscription at Ilkley. This later associated with *OS haefr* winding and made into Hwerf the river Wharfe.

Aire: The river Aire once formed the southern boundary of the Liberty at Baildon. Like many rivers names it is of British origin from the *OC isara* ' the strong river.

Danefield: *OE dene* 'valley'. There is no evidence that the Danes had anything to do with this name. This part of Yorkshire came under the influence of Mercia prior to 662 AD and *dan* is the Mercian form of the Anglian *dene* or 'valley'. The course of the Holbeck must have been the valley and the field the land on each side but the name is now only used for wood.

Kirkgate: Kirkgate has a very long history as a road for it was part of the prehistoric track across the valley which used the ford across the Wharfe. It must have been the way to worship and to market even in early Anglian times. For the earliest Anglian is now dated 675 – 700 AD. Kirk is *ON* for 'church' and gate meant a 'way, a road', Kirkgate must date from the earliest Norse settlement.

Bondgate: Bondgate is derived from the *OE bondi* meaning boundman or bondman, one who is tied to the soil and who was bound to render service to his Lord. Bondgate must have been laid out when Otley became a town as the dwelling place for those bondmen who were denied the privileges of living in the town. The market charter was granted in 1222 and Bondgate was outside the bounds of the town at that time. There is a Bondgate in Ripon, Appleby, Westmorland which is mentioned in 1292. These instances suggests that Bondgate's were a development of late Norman times.

Caley: *OE calu* 'bare', 'bald', *ley* 'an open space'. Caley was probably a hamlet now represented by a farm, the Hall has recently been pulled down. To the south are rock cliffs which were the *Calu* or 'bare place' overlooking the *ley* or 'open area'.

Northgate: Bearing in mind that gate was the Norse term for a 'road', the name is self-explanatory. Northgate led to the ford over the river Wharfe where

the breach in the morraine afforded a good approach and a firm bottom to the river. This was the best crossing in twenty miles and ultimately the reason that Otley became a market town. Except for the old Hall, Northgate, now Bridge Street, was without houses until recent times.

Menston: The earliest form of Menston was *Mesindon* and a little later *Mensington*, the *OE tun* was a 'fenced enclosure', the *ing* meant 'the place of settlement of', *Men* represented *Mensa*, an early chieftain. An early rendering of the name might be 'place of the people of *Mensa*'.

Burras: *ME bur* 'a burdock'. Although Burras Lane is the name we know now, the names of enclosure date show the whole area to the south was known as Burras or 'The Burdocks'.

Gay Lane: Here we have the *ON geil*, 'a ravine' becoming *gale* and finally *gay* 'lane' is the *OE lanu*, 'a lane'. The ravines or ravine were the sunken ways cut by pack horse tracks across the slopes of the Chevin. These are still to be seen below the Old Leeds Road. The sunken road below Stainburn Church is still known as the Gayles.

Lisker: *OE laes*, 'a pasture', *ON kiarr* 'swampy wood, a marsh'. This name, The Marsh Pastures, is truly descriptive. It is the lowest part of the lowlands and still swampy.

1800 – 1900

For centuries, Otley remained in the same social and economic condition: a small self-contained rural township with a very slow growing population; there were only 2,332 people in 1800. Crafts, trades and occupations were unchanged from preceding centuries with tanners, fellmongers, curriers, saddlers and cordwainers (leather); joiners, carpenters, chairmakers, coopers, cartwrights, wheelwrights and cloggers, (in wood); the blacksmith, whitesmith, tinners and ironmongers, farmers, millers, maltsters, bakers, butchers, masons and chandlers, combers, weavers, clothiers and of course, carriers, innkeepers and ostlers.

At the beginning of 1800, the town possessed a corn mill, paper mill, skinning mill and four flax mills in West Gill, (later known as Hell Hole Gill due to the working conditions there), since renamed Ellar Gill. Although the worsted industry did not come to Otley until the early nineteenth century, combing, spinning and serge weaving had been carried on for a long time in individual cottages.

William Ackroyd was quite young when in 1820 he purchased part of the skinning sheds in Ilkley Road from Daniel Forster. In 1836 he took into partnership a Scotsman, Thomas Duncan, whose sons James and Thomas took over control of the business on the death of William Ackroyd in 1865. Rather surprisingly, water wheels were in use here until 1884, when one was replaced by a turbine, and by 1890 the remaining water wheels were demolished.

In 1880, control of the mill known locally as Duncan's Mill, was in the hands of John, Thomas Arthur and James Hastings and Albany Duncan, remaining so until 1919 when the last three were partners and formed a limited company. It was during this period the mill employed over 1,000 persons then known as 'hands'. Thomas died in 1925, being succeeded by his sons Kenneth and Harold, and Sir James Hastings Duncan MP (knighted in 1914) was followed in the business by his son Hugh. Control of the company eventually passed to Edward H Wolfe, the son of Dr. H and Mrs Wolfe (the daughter of Sir James) and Ronald H Duncan MA, JP, the son of Col. Hugh Duncan, thus the family is one of two existing businesses in the town with continuity in the same family.

Between 1830-40 the new road to Bradford was built, cutting through the deep ravine of West Gill superseding the two old tracks via East Chevin and Hunger Hill. About the same time, proposals were being made and sums of money advanced by the firms of Hartley (corn mill), Garnett (paper mill), and Ackroyd (textile) towards the cost of a new road to Leeds which would avoid the steep road up East Chevin. The new road was opened in 1842.

The population of the town doubled between 1800 and 1860 due to two facts: the potato famine of 1845 in Ireland and the resultant influx of Irish immigrants in 1847, and the introduction of the printing machine engineering industry in the middle of the century.

Opposite: Eric Wood, Blacksmith (copyright Winpenny Photography).

This industry indirectly begins with William Walker, the prolific market town printer who published a huge range of cheap, popular literature during the century and beyond. His talented sons continued the business and started the Wharfedale Observer in 1880. It was William Walker who first asked William Dawson, a joiner, to make simple machinery to aid the printing trade. In 1850, Dawson, in co-operation with David Payne also a joiner and skilful inventive mechanic, was responsible for converting the cutting machines of wood into machines of iron and by 1845 they had perfected the 'Wharfedale' printing machine.

There was great expansion in the machine industry during the next 40 years, first with the Wharfedale Iron Works in 1863, later known as the Bremner Machine Company, in Side Copse, and followed by Robert Elliott, an iron founder who made the iron castings required by Dawson. In 1865, Dawson built his own foundry and began making his own castings which resulted in Elliot joining with John Fieldhouse and John Kelley, former employees of Dawson, but in 1887 Elliott began his own business in Gay Lane with machines under the name of 'the Defiance'.

Fieldhouse, Crossfield and Company were next on the scene in 1865, making their 'Reliance' machines in premises in Nelson Street. David Payne, previously in partnership with Dawson, began his own business in 1866; Waite and Saville in Burras Lane in 1893, their machines being the 'Falcon'; John Kelley in Leeds Road in 1896, and J W Potter in 1902, in premises at the bottom of Silver Mill Hill once owned by Messrs. Kidd – the Freehold Act Metal Works. Finally, John Kay, who served his apprenticeship under William Dawson, built his small work in Westgate (the Century Buildings) making his own machines. This business closed during the depression of 1926-30. The detailed story of Otley's printers' engineers is told in 'Otley and the Wharfedale Printing Machine' by Paul Wood.

Tanning was still an important industry during the nineteenth century as, in addition to Daniel Forster in Ilkley Road, there were the tanneries and bark mills of Denbigh and Young, and drying sheds in Station Road. Robert Barker moved to new premises in Cross Green, relinquished tanning and began a leather-dressing business, with additional premises in Gay Lane, the last named being sold in 1931.

The success of the these firms was made possible by the opening up of the town to the large industrial towns to the south by the two new roads and the arrival of the railway system in 1865 which linked Otley with Bradford, Ilkley and Harrogate.

As a result of the increased population during the century under review, 6,898 between 1801 and 1904, it was inevitable that more accommodation would be required to house the intake of newcomers. Earlier, houses had been built sporadically within the confines of the medieval burgage area, in back yards and back gardens, and it was not until about 1845-55 that the common fields of the town were encroached upon and the large scale building of long rows of houses really began. Kays Crescent, Ashfield Place and Peels Crescent being the first, all in close proximity to the textile mill, followed in 1865-70 to the east of the town in the Side Copse area: South View and West View Terraces,

Danefield and Grosvenor Terraces, St Claire Street, Bremner Street and Bermondsey Street. In the years 1877-79, Cambridge Allotment, mostly orchards adjoining Gay Lane, was built up, with Orchard Street and Carlton Street (houses at £195 each), Fairfax Street, Cambridge (from £460 to £490 each) and East View Terrace (£745 each). A few years later saw the building of Albion Street, South Parade and Craven Street and to the west, the Granville area, and near the end of the century North Avenue, North Street, Ramsey Terrace and Hamilton Terrace were built on the fields near Back Lane.

In the nineteenth century some larger buildings such as the Salem Chapel in Bridge Street in 1825, replaced by the present building in 1899 (now the Bridge Church). The Wesleyan Chapel in Boroughgate was also built in 1825, but is not now in use, as the Methodists in 1875 decided on a new chapel: the present one in Boroughgate. The Primitive Methodists had a small building in Newmarket Street in 1833, moving to a new chapel in Station Road in 1874. The Roman Catholic Church dates from 1850, having been built at the expense of Mr Thomas Constable of the Manor House. The United Methodist community built an imposing chapel in Westgate in 1856, which was demolished in the middle of the twentieth century.

The Fire Brigade was formed in 1866, followed by the Militia (Royal Engineers) and the military band which became known as Otley Band.

All the sporting and social clubs were formed during this century, the first appears to have been the Cricket Club, who were playing matches with Knaresborough, Wetherby, Woodhouse and others as early as 1820. The Philharmonic Society came into existence in 1848, the Parish Church Choir formed in 1867 and in the following year the Otley Choral Union. Football has been played for many years but not on any organised footing and the earliest known club was the Rugby Union about 1874 who won the Yorkshire Challenge Cup in 1889. The Association Football clubs in the town included the White Star, Clarence, Cambridge, Wesley, White Rose, Parish Church, Mechanics Institute and the Otley AFC, who at the turn of the century were playing in the Bradford League. The Angling Club was founded in 1874 and the Athletic Society in 1878, the Amateur Dramatic Society in the same year and round about 1890-92, the formation of the Otley Road Club (who by 1904 has become the Otley Cycling Club with HQ in Boroughgate). In the 90's the following were formed: Otley Harriers, St Joseph's RU Club and the Otley and District Tennis and Bowling Club in Westgate.

Right: Otley Mills

Otley as A Market Town

Otley has officially been a market town for 780 years, King Henry III having granted a Royal Charter for the first time in 1222 A.D. when he put the control of the market in the hands of the Archbishop of York, and the Archbishop's representative collected a small charge or 'toll' on all items brought to Otley for sale.

In the early days a regular market for dry goods and produce took place, often on Sundays in the church yard, or even in the church itself in bad weather, but livestock was traded in the main streets and in the yards of the numerous public houses which then existed in the town. There were special Fairs on certain Saints' days during the year, at which large numbers of livestock were traded.

At the time of the Civil War in the mid 1600s significant changes took place and the regular market trading moved to Cross Green where it was based until 1800, when the site for the stalls was transferred again, on that occasion to its present location in the Market Place. In 1800 the market place boasted an old timber 'shambles', but there were no shops concentrated around it. The old timber 'shambles' was cleared away in 1872.

Otley was well served with transport, as there was a frequent coach service along the Doncaster to Kendal main road, which passed through the town, and the horses were often changed here.

Following the invention of Tarmacadam in 1845, there was a general move to improve road surfaces, and Otley was no exception. The railway system was extended to the town in 1865, and in 1885 the government ordered the removal of animal markets away from the centres of all market towns, to 'off street sites', thus leaving the thoroughfares much cleaner for pedestrians and uncluttered for vehicles, which until the early 1900s were still mainly horse drawn.

In the late 1800s two firms of auctioneers set up 'off street' livestock auction marts in the town. Mr. J. W. Dacre began in Station Road and later moved to the foot of East Chevin Road, the Station Road mart then being run by Joseph Horner until about 1895 when Joseph Lister bought those premises. For a short time between 1928 and 1933 the two businesses were amalgamated and run as one, but by 1935 a second market was again in operation at new premises just north of Otley Bridge. That market gained nationwide recognition for the town as a dairy cattle market after the Second World War, and for a quarter of a century it became the premier market in the country for that type of business.

But, as the twentieth century came to an end, farming prosperity declined, and in January 2000 the Bridge End market closed down, leaving just the one livestock auction mart, Wharfedale Farmers', to serve the local farming community. In fact, although several market towns throughout the country had, during the twentieth century, boasted

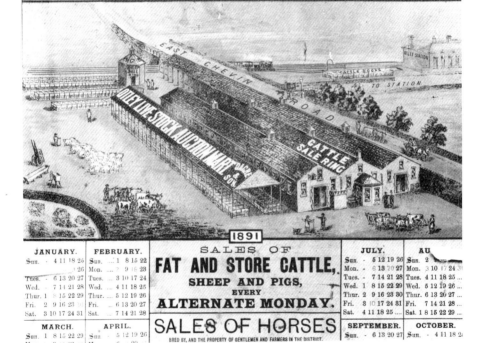

two livestock auction marts, Otley was the last town in England to maintain two.

Changing farming circumstances and the growth of the use of electronic communications are leading to significant changes in the manner in which farmers' business is transacted; but there is a considerable wealth of expertise within the town which will ensure the continuing vigour of Otley as an agricultural centre during the twenty-first century.

Agriculture In Wharfedale

Otley enjoys an enviable and unrivalled location in terms of potential for agricultural business. It lies on the southern edge of the ancient 'Forest of Knaresborough', no longer a forest but, during most of the past 1,000 years, a heavily wooded area. Today we have mainly arable land for 65 miles to the east, and with higher rainfall areas of grassland and dairy farming extending continuously for 65 miles to the west with narrow dales, heather moorland and no sizeable towns in the 100 miles north of Otley. There is a population greater than that of London and therefore a massive consuming area, in the region that begins just over the top of the Chevin, extending 50 miles south.

The area's agriculture has had mixed fortunes. The two main periods of dramatic expansion have been the eras of George III and Elizabeth II. Until the early 1600s, farming here was largely under the control of the Church. The monks of Bolton Abbey farmed most of the cleared land in the lower Wharfe valley, from Harewood in the east to Greenfield westwards.

Then followed the turbulence of the Civil War, but for 50 years from 1750 remarkable improvements were made: wooded areas were cleared, common grazing on moorlands were divided up and given to individual farmers to cultivate. The majority of the stone walls which are to be seen today in the higher parts of our locality were built during that period, and considerable improvements were made in livestock breeding.

Two wealthy local men, Henry Carr Ibbetson of Denton Hall and Fison of Greenholme, Burley in Wharfedale, are credited with the development of the celebrated Shorthorn breed of cattle which became one of the principal breeds throughout the country for the next century or so. The same two men were instrumental in founding Wharfedale Agricultural Society in 1796.

From the early 1800s, control of farming land in this valley was in the hands of the landed gentry and the wealthy industrialists who arrived as a result of the industrial revolution of the 1840s. Many of the farmsteads which we see around Otley today were constructed or re-constructed as a result of their fortune in the reign of Queen Victoria. Local farmers did not find much financial success during the period from 1850 to 1950, despite the world wars, because the government increasingly chose to import food from abroad, whenever it could find a source cheaper than at home, without any regard for the long term health of British agriculture.

The interruption of shipping and food supplies during the second world war did demonstrate to government that home food production was vital and, during the next forty years, government financial support allowed British farmers to feed the nation with food of the highest quality but at the lower prices which competed with the cost of foreign imports, to the benefit of all of the population. Farmers, almost without exception, were able to make many improvements such as re-modelling their farm buildings so that mechanisation could improve efficiency; re-draining land to improve its capacity to yield more; and re-fencing fields allowing fields the more efficient use of tractors and machinery. These changes can be seen all around Otley. By the time of Queen Elizabeth's Silver Jubilee in 1977 the whole of the rural surroundings clearly gave an appearance of prosperity and of ongoing progress.

The last twenty years or so have seen a gradual and accelerating decline taking place again, and the rural areas of Wharfedale have not escaped. Not all farm land looks as well kept as it did because agriculture is suffering.

All farmers, for most of the past twenty years, have been compelled by government to cut back their production by around 20% below the levels of the early 1980s. In the early 1990s the cattle breeding industry suffered from the ravages of the cattle disease BSE and, as a direct consequence, the export of beef from the United Kingdom was banned with the result that the value of beef farmers' output fell by 24%. The government has ordered, since early 1996, that all of the nation's breeding cattle have to be killed and the carcasses incinerated at the end of their breeding life. Although some compensation is available, farmers have suffered a cut in income of around 37% for these animals. Government has, once again, forgotten the vital necessity for self-sufficiency in food production, and has resorted to a cheap imported food policy to the neglect of British agriculture.

Hence the countryside around Otley is changing . The landscape which we prize is not only the natural landscape; a large part is entirely man made, and has been farmer maintained during the past 200 years. Today all arable land has areas of compulsory 'setaside' within it and such areas are growing wild. The imposition of 'quotas' upon livestock farmers is inexorably leading to a less profitable, more untidy and less manicured form of countryside management, and this trend seems set to continue for some time.

Wharfeside Mills - Garnetts

Mills have operated on the site of the present Wharfeside Mills from very early times. With information from authentic sources along with site evidence, there is a complete picture of the area, but space permits only a brief history. The first mention of a mill on the site is in the Pipe Rolls of Richard I, dated 1195-1196, at the time a corn mill was leased from the Archbishop of York, Lord of the Manor of Otley. It remained in that usage for the next 600 years. From 1535 the mill was also used for 'fulling' - a process used on woollen cloth where the cloth was put into pits full of human urine and workers would walk on it to thicken it and give a matted finish. This practice gave us the name Walkergate, where the fullers actually lived.

This is the earliest evidence of a textile trade being carried out in Otley. Originally, the mill was probably worked from a small mill pond adjacent to the river, where the present football field is. By 1677, there was a small dam across the river, a quarter the length of the present one. Paper making was introduced in 1722, by which time there were three mills devoted to corn, fulling and paper making. After the lengthening of the bridge in 1775, a larger dam was built in 1872, which still exists today.

Jeremiah Garnett became connected with the mill in 1783, the start of a family association lasting over 150 years. In 1806, Jeremiah retired and his son William took over the running of the mill. William's son Peter joined the business in the early 1820s and he founded the company name. The first reference to Peter Garnett & Sons is in Salter's Directory of 1855, and five years later simply P Garnett & Son. In 1865, Peter died, leaving his son Jeremiah with the option to buy the mill. The Garnett family owned the mill until 1935 when they sold their interests to Associated Paper. 1n 1990 Chandaria Industries acquired the mill and approximately 200 people are currently employed, producing between 350 and 400 tonnes of specialist paper each week.

From Textile Mills To Business Centre – William Ackroyd (Holdings) Limited

For at least 200 years textile activity (cotton spinning, fulling, wool combing and worsted spinning) was continuous at Otley Mills until in 1983 trading ceased. The wool textile industry in Yorkshire, long in decline, succumbed to competition from developing countries. Five generations of the Duncan Family had built on the foundations laid by William Ackroyd who began worsted spinning in 1815 and took on Thomas Duncan from Scotland as partner. By the 1880s the mills employed over 1000 people and the prosperity of the company resulted in the construction of a massive new mill, Pegholme, opened in 1889.

Because the seven-acre Otley Mills site belonged to the company, new buildings could be added without the need for demolishing the old: so the stock of buildings, many under-used or redundant, spanned from mid 1780 to the late nineteenth century. Technological advances telescoped the number of processes involved in spinning and weaving. The need to specialise meant that instead of starting from the sheep's back and ending at the finished cloth the company concentrated on two or three intermediate processes. At the same time fewer and fewer employees were needed to produce vastly increased output. But not even the introduction of revolutionary new machinery and round-the-clock working saved the situation. Nationwide, the textile industry was in structural decline. William Ackroyd and Company Limited ceased trading and closed its doors in 1983.

However, that grim necessity left a heritage of mill buildings: architecturally varied, historically important and ripe for rescue and conversion but, sadly, no capital available to finance the refurbishment because efforts to remain afloat as a company had exhausted the reserves.

Over the last 18 years, slowly and at first painfully, the company has converted one building after another for post-industrial activities, recently concentrating on office development. The Wharfebank Business Centre now houses some 55 enterprises employing between 400 to 500 people. There is a full house and a waiting list of prospective tenants eager to occupy an out-of-city riverside location within 10 miles of Leeds and Bradford. An old redundant mill has become a showpiece office complex for twenty-first century service industry.

Education

In the sixteenth century, much of the available education was provided by the numerous monasteries, which had been established in England during the previous centuries. With the dissolution of the monasteries, these opportunities became fewer. However, many people of standing began to sponsor grammar schools mainly for the sons of gentlemen, but they were also open to boys from poorer homes at little or no charge. Thomas Cave, a citizen of Otley, was such a person. He generously left £250 for the founding of such a school on condition that the people of Otley should provide a similar amount, and that the school should be founded within four years of his death.

James I granted the first Royal Charter for the school, in the name of his son, the Prince of Wales, in 1607, but it was to be a further four years before the school which was to become Prince Henry's Grammar School opened its doors for the first time. This document is proudly held by the school and the feathers from the crest form part of the school badge. The Grammar School was brought into use in 1614, partly funded by rent received from land bought by the Governors in Northallerton. Records dated 1819 show that there were 30 pupils registered at the school. Seven years later, 43 pupils were enrolled, three of whom were receiving a free classical education. By this time, there were eight other schools serving the needs of the town. In 1840 the building was altered to its present form, the Governors earned extra income by letting the premises for use as the Magistrates Court. The school appeared to be popular and by 1851 there were 104 boys on its roll. Ten years later with only 30 pupils and debts of £120, the doors closed until 1865 when it re-opened again with a different fee paying structure. Sadly by 1874, possibly against competition from the Collegiate School in Burras Lane, it closed its doors once again.

Before the great Education Acts of the 19th century, schooling in Otley, as in the rest of the country, was provided by small fee paying schools and by the voluntary sector but there was no compulsion to attend. The only education for poor children was available through the churches initially in Sunday Schools and later in sectarian schools. The National Society for Promoting the Education of the Poor in the Principles of the Established Church was a prominent body and one of the first recipients in 1833, of education grants given by the government From this source, the National School in Cross Green was built in 1847 and later the Infants School in Wharfe Street was opened.

In 1918, forty-four years after it had closed its doors, Prince Henry's School once again became part of the education scene in Otley when it opened in the Mechanics Institute in temporary classrooms until the buildings on the present site were completed in 1925.

Local firms provided scholarships to supplement the free places based on the 'eleven-plus' examination of the former West Riding County Council. At this time PHGS became a co-educational school. In 1936, senior pupils transferred to the Old Board School renamed North Parade Secondary Modern.

The Roman Catholic community was swelled by many Irish immigrants who came to

THE OLD GRAMMAR SCHOOL, OTLEY.

Otley and settled in an area which become known as the Irish fields. They were fortunate in having the Constable family who lived in The Manor House as benefactors. Mr Thomas Constable had built the church on Bridge Street and his chaplain taught the children in the Priest's House alongside.

As the Roman Catholic numbers increased, Miss M Constable, who lived in Dovecote House on Boroughgate, bought land in Crow Lane and paid for a school to be built here in 1861. Ten years later a further block was added to accommodate the rising numbers. This building served the Roman Catholic population until 1964. At this time, senior pupils transferred to a new school St Mary's Secondary School in Menston. The Crow Lane school continued for infant and junior pupils until 1969 when a new school was opened on land next to the Manor House. Sadly the original school, after a time as a scrapyard, is now in a dilapidated state of repair and unused.

Nineteenth century legislation required that children working in mills and factories must receive part-time education and thus a small 'mill' school was built in Ilkley Road in 1871. Later a larger block was added. Mill workers and their children were educated here. Ackroyd's the mill owners sold the school to the School Broad in 1882. Thus began the life of Westgate School which was an all-age school until 1936 when senior pupils transferred to North Parade Secondary School. Westgate became a First School in 1969. This fine old building will continue to serve Otley families for many years to come, this time as a junior school in the recent re-organisation of Otley schools.

The 1870 Education Act established education for all children of elementary age and School Boards were set up to administer and provide schools. The Otley Board opened the first board school in 1880 in North Parade. Children who wanted to work full time had to sit an examination in order to be able to do so, sitting the exam at the North Parade School. St Joseph's had 14 part-timers in 1920.

After many years of public pressure, North Parade School was organised as a senior school in 1936 for pupils who had not gained the '11 plus' examination. In 1969, it became a Junior and Infants School; seven years later the old 'Board' school was re-organised into the All Saints Middle School as a part of the Local Education Authority's new 'three tier' concept in education. The most recent LEA re-organisation has been unable to find a place for this historic school which has served many generations of Otley families and so it closes its doors after 122 years of service to the town.

In the quarter century since 1977 the schools in our town have continued to provide quality educational experiences for the families in the town as well as the neighbouring areas. However, a decline in the numbers of children of school age, along with national changes brought about by various Acts of Parliament, will make a considerable impact on the number and type of schools compared with those that existed in 1977. The local authority announced the changes in 1997 and invited parents to consider them. Basically, some schools would close their doors for good, while others were to change the age ranges of their pupils and new buildings and extensions would be needed to accommodate the proposed changes. Meetings were held by the Local Education Authority with groups of parents, staff and School Governors prior to the final announcement. The plans have not been without their critics: some parents were satisfied with the plans whilst others were less pleased.

Ashfield (opened 1972), will become a 4-11 year old school, extensions needed.

Thomas Chippendale formerly Weston Lane (opened 1953), will close.

The Whartons (opened 1975), will continue as a 4-11 year school.

Westgate (opened 1879), will become a 4-11 year school, extensions needed.

Lisker Drive (opened 1976), will become a 4-11 year school, extensions needed.

All Saints Junior (opened 1879), formerly the 'Modern School', will close.

St Joseph's Roman Catholic School (opened 1861), will continue as a 4-11 year old school.

Prince Henry's Comprehensive School (opened 1927), will continue as an 11-18 year school.

Newall Infant School (1936 to 1995) continues to be used by Prince Henry's Grammar School as a Language College since 1997.

In addition to these schools some of which have a nursery on site, provision for pre-school education is available at several church and private centres in the town.

Evening classes have been a feature of education in Otley for many years as vocational and academic groups followed their particular interests in the various locations within the town. Students come from all age groups to pursue their hobbies or study for public examinations or certificates. Park Lane College, with its main site in Leeds, has opened a branch in Bondgate complete with IT courses and computer suite.

The Manor House

The Manor House was built about 1792 by Matthew Wilson, a lawyer and kinsman of the Reverend T F Wilson of Burley Hall, who was Vicar of Weston 1795-1803. It is situated in the grounds of the former medieval Manor House of the Archbishop of York, owned by William Snell of Otley, Attorney at Law.

In the Land Assessments for 1801, Matthew Wilson was assessed at the sum of 19/10d for the House, Hall Garth and Little Hall Garth. On his death in 1826 he was succeeded by his son, Henry, who sold the property in 1829 to John Smith, Solicitor of Otley.

In 1836, Thomas Angus Constable, lawyer and solicitor, bought the Manor House and grounds with other copyhold property, which included Dovecote House in Boroughgate. His sister, Miss Mary Constable, moved into Dovecote House. Thomas Constable, a member of an ancient Yorkshire county family and under steward of the Manor of Otley, married Elizabeth Ducarel, daughter of the Marquis de la Pasture. Their only daughter, Mary, married Charles B.J. Stourton of Allerton Park, near Knaresborough. He was the 24th Baron Mowbray, 25th Baron Seagrave and 21st Baron Stourton – Lord Mowbray and Stourton, Premier Baron of England. Thomas Constable added Clitherow House to the side of the Manor House to act as an office for meeting clients and collecting rates. He died in 1891 at the age of 86.

After the death of Elizabeth Constable in 1919, the Manor House was used for various purposes, one being the headquarters of the Otley Derby Sweepstake, which became quite notorious at the time.

Mary, Lady Mowbray and Stourton, on the death of her husband in 1936, left Allerton Park, Knaresborough, and again took up residence at the Manor House until her death in December 1961 at the age of 91. Her daughter, the Hon. Charlotte Stourton, resided at the Manor House until moving to Harrogate in the late 1970s where she still lives. The Manor House was leased and some of the grounds sold to the Harewood Housing Trust for sheltered housing.

Churches

Churches together in Otley

Until the introduction of Methodism to Otley in the 1750s, the Parish Church would have been the centre of religious activity in the town. During the reformation in England the monarch replaced the Pope as head of the Church but the organisation remained episcopal (administered by Bishops), as was the Roman Church.

By the 1920s, a multiplicity of religious groups had settled and built churches in the town.

A detailed historical study of Otley would probably show the influence of the rise of Methodism on the community of Otley in the eighteenth century and the effect of the influx of the Roman Catholics from Ireland in the nineteenth century.

In the 1960s and 1970s the present day United Reformed and Methodists were formed and in 1966 most of the churches agreed to work together within the organisation of the Otley Council of Churches. The following Churches and groups are now part of the organisation, which changed its name in 2001 to the Churches Together in Otley - United Reformed Church, Methodist, Salvation Army, Roman Catholic, Church of England, Quaker and New Life.

There have been many spiritual initiatives from the Churches Together over the years including special unity services, processions, and Songs of Praise on the first Saturday of each month. At Easter in 1992 the churches presented a community street play called Son Rise which was written and produced by local people. Currently members from all churches come together for breakfast and prayer on the first Saturday of each month.

In the 1980s groups of people from all the churches met for study at Lent and at other times and were well prepared for the changes in Church Unity structures in 1989 linked with the Swanwick Declaration, in which the leaders of all the churches at national level made a commitment to work together more than previously. For many years the local church ministers have meet on a regular basis for mutual support and to check that they are, where possible, fulfilling the needs of the people of the town. In addition to the wit-

---

Church Activity in Otley

c1200: Archbishop's palace near site of RC church *c800:* Parish church built

1517: Reformation *1730:* Start of Methodism *1759:* Methodist chapel at Green Lane built

1771: Methodist chapel at Nelson Street built *1821:* Congregationalists came to Otley

1825: Methodist Church in Boroughgate built *1826:* Congregationalists built Salem Chapel *1833:* The Methodist Primitives built Newmarket Chapel *1851:* Roman Catholic Church built *1857:* Methodist church in Westgate built *1878:* Salvation Army formed

1874: Methodist Chapel rebuilt in Boroughgate *1882:* Salvation Army came to Otley

1899: Duncan Cathedral replaced the Salem Chapel *1916:* Formation of Bethel from Methodism *1920:* Bethel settled in Mercury Row *1923:* Salvation Army moved to Newmarket *1932:* Primitive & New Connection joined *1965:* Methodist congregations unite *1965:* Chevin Cross made *1972:* Formation of the United Reformed Church

1973: Bethel moved above Senior Citizens Club *1966:* Formation of Otley Council of Christian Churches *1999:-2000:* New Chevin Cross put up for Millennium Celebrations

2001: Otley Council of Christian Churches renamed as Churches Together in Otley.

ness of voluntary work carried out by many Christians in the town, the Churches Together has been active on many practical levels in the town as well as being represented on other town organisations.

The cross on the Chevin, which was installed for the first time in 1969, has now become a well known and loved Easter symbol of hope. The cross, which was replaced after 31 years for the new millennium, was the brainchild of the Otley Council of Christian Churches and is a fine example of a co-operative initiative, which has become a source of comfort and inspiration to many people.

The divisions of the past can still be seen in the differences of detailed theology and practice between the churches, however there is an understanding by each church that all are journeying in the same direction, albeit on different routes. The variations between the churches are seen as offering creative choice for people in their search for God.

Bridge United Reformed Church

The Society of Independents (or Congregationalists) was formed in Otley in 1821, first meeting for worship in the Assembly Rooms above the Bowling Green pub in Bondgate. The members of the Society were a mixture of native Otley people and Scottish drapers who had settled in the town. In 1825 they moved for a short time to a room behind the Black Bull (The Pump Chapel).

In 1826 they opened their first purpose-built chapel, Salem Chapel, in Bridge Street, and soon called their first minister, Rev. James Swift Hastie, who was minister for nearly 50 years. A Sunday School was built to the rear in 1835 and the chapel extended in 1856. Many of Otley's industrialists were members and the growth of the town because of that industry necessitated newer and larger buildings. A new hall and Sunday School were opened on new land to the rear in 1882 and the new Otley Congregational Church was opened in 1899 on the site of the old chapel. These are the buildings we see today. The hall was rebuilt following a major fire in 1993.

In 1972 the majority of Congregational Churches united with the Presbyterian Church in England and became the United Reformed Church, the Otley church adopting the name of 'The Bridge Church'.

The Bridge Church offers many activities for young people including Beavers, Cubs, Brownies, Scouts, Guides, and Pilots. Central to all its activities is worship as the church responds to the spiritual needs of the town.

Methodists

Methodism sprang up in Otley around 1740, largely due to the impassioned preaching of John Nelson, a stonemason from Birstall. The road in front of the Post Office still bears his name.

The early Methodists met first at Green Lane near the old railway line and then built their first chapel on the site of HSBC in Nelson Street in 1771. John Wesley, the

founder of Methodism, was to preach here and to visit Otley on a score of occasions during his tireless journeys on horseback round the country. He developed a warm friendship with the Ritchie family and a plaque may be seen outside their former home in Boroughgate.

Methodist numbers grew phenomenally and a bigger Chapel was built in 1825, now part of Chevin Court. Finally, the present Chapel was erected in Boroughgate in 1875 with a seating capacity of 1000.

Offshoots from the main Wesleyan movement began to appear in Otley in the nineteenth century. 'The New Connexion' Methodists built a Chapel in Walkergate and a later one in Westgate, now a car park. The Primitive Methodists built a Chapel, now the Salvation Army Citadel, and a larger one in Station Road. There were also two Mission Halls, the Craven Street Mission and the Otley and Wharfedale Mission. From the latter sprang the Bethel Gospel Mission.

Following the two world wars church attendances dwindled and by 1965 all Methodists in Otley were meeting at the main Church in Boroughgate. In the early seventies the Church was modernised, introducing glass doors at the front and a large foyer. Ceilings were lowered and the sanctuary redecorated.

At the present time an ambitious redevelopment scheme has been launched which includes plans for better access at the rear of the Church as well as better amenities for young folk and the disabled. The Methodist Church in Otley now has fewer than 200 members, but apart from worship services, its premises are well used by many and varied groups and organisations.

For over 250 years the Methodist people have worshipped and served the community of Otley. It is our hope that we will continue to serve Jesus as his disciples well into the twenty-first century.

Our Lady and All Saints Roman Catholic Church

The Church celebrated its 150th anniversary on 24th June 2001 having being built by Thomas Constable in 1851 in the grounds of the Manor House at a cost of £4,000. Ten years later, the west end of the church was added.

During the 1840's, a number of Irish families were invited by Thomas Constable to live in Otley to escape the ravages of the Irish Potato Famine. They initially were settled in tents on what has become known as Irish Fields. With the increase in the number of Roman Catholic people in Otley, the church was built to eliminate the seven mile trek to Middleton Lodge, Ilkley every Sunday to celebrate Mass. A number of the Irish people arrived starving, with famine-related diseases and the young particularly suffered

with a number dying soon after their arrival in Otley. In 2001, a memorial stone was positioned in the outside of the south wall of the church to commemorate the burial of some 50 people in the grounds of the Parish Church. At that time, there was no consecrated ground in Otley for Roman Catholic burials.

OUR LADY AND ALL SAINTS · OTLEY

A number of refurbishments have been carried out through the history of the Church, the last being in 1992/3. A new altar similar in design to the original altar was installed in the sanctuary and the sanctuary roof renewed. A new window, designed by Ann Sotheran, was put into the East end of the church and the old window moved to the west wall. The statue of Our Lady was moved to her own chapel at the rear of the church. The baptismal font was repositioned with a new tabernacle for baptismal oils placed in the wall nearby.

Otley New Life Church

Otley New Life Church started in 1993, meeting in the rooms above Beks in Kirkgate. There were about 40 people at that time including adults and children, with Paul Lancaster as the leader of the church. The church was a plant out from Aireborough Community Church. Since 1993 they have moved their venue three times, using different locations in Otley: first to the Salvation Army, then to the Civic Centre, before their current location in Mercury Row. They have distributed mince pies at Christmas time to street traders and shopkeepers as well as handing out hot cross buns in the street over Easter with explanatory leaflets.

They also financially support missionaries living currently in Azerbijan and Thailand. For the past two years there has been a Christian youth event at the skateboard park. This is set to continue annually. We'd like to host other youth events across the town in conjunction with other churches. Their desire for the future is to make a greater impact on the youth of Otley and have more involvement in the local community.

Salvation Army

The basis of this movement came when its founder William Booth was to leave the Primative Methodist group in 1865 to devote his work to the spiritual healing amongst the poor and deprived in the East End of London. He found little success in old methods, hence assisted by his wife he established a quasi-military organisation in 1878.

In 1882 a band of three score soldiers 'invaded and captured' Otley under the command of Major Cadman. A local command was established in an old leather factory by the pole. It was the 73rd corps led by Mr W Hodgson. Within a week the premises were converted into a barracks to accommodate 750. Three weeks later the building was destroyed by arson except for the ground floor which was saved by the fire service. In the 1870s the Methodist Chapel in Newmarket became vacant and in 1923 became the Salvation Army Citadel. The Jubilee year of 1935 saw the Commander in Chief 'General Evangeline Booth' pass through Otley. The newspaper reports tremendous crowds which slowed her passage, giving her an opportunity to speak to many people of Otley.

The suite of buildings was completely refurbished in 1995. In co-operation with other Christians, we seek to meet the needs of the local communities in a balanced programme of social and spiritual help.

To provide an open environment of open-hearted acceptance that will enable, support and nurture the spiritual growth and social well-being of all, regardless of age, sex, race, class or creed.

Quakers

There have been Quakers living in Otley and Wharfedale for the last 350 years. Properly known as members of the Religious Society of Friends, many derived from a network of dales folk called Seekers, who were inspired to follow the radical thoughts of George Fox in the early 1650s.

These included a philosophy of non-violence, and that we should work to do away with all wars while pursuing equality, truth and simplicity in our daily lives. These beliefs caused a lot of hardship for Quakers then and still do today! Many Friends were imprisoned either for refusing to pay church tithes, to swear allegiance to the Crown or to swear on the bible in court.

In 1665 there were only four Quaker 'public' Meeting houses in Yorkshire (Thirsk, Settle, Scarborough and Askwith, near Otley), so Quakers usually held their silent m meetings for worship in private houses. Following the Toleration Act of 1689, houses could be licensed for Worship and Otley Quakers went to one of these in either Otley or Askwith.

The first meeting house in Otley was built at Cross Green in 1776 and Askwith Quakers went to Otley when Askwith Meeting closed in 1778. The site at Cross Green was let to the Plymouth Brethren in the mid-nineteenth century, and the arrangement continues as there is a Quaker burial ground on the site. There have been Quaker Meetings in Otley for the past 20 years, at first in homes then later in the Otley Cycle Club premises in Wellbeck. Currently, thanks to the Methodists, we meet in the church parlour in Boroughgate.

Scouting in Otley

Scouting had a very early beginning in Otley, so it may be useful to start with some relevant details of the movement as a whole.

1907: Robert Baden-Powell took 20 boys to camp on Brownsea Island in Poole Harbour.

1908: B-P published the first copy of *Scouting for Boys* – at about the same time the first issue of *The Scout* magazine came out which spread the word far and wide.

1909: The Scouting HQ was established in Victoria Street, London. King Edward VII knighted B-P. By 1909 some lads were forming patrols in Otley.

1911: Sea Scouts came into existence.

1916: Wolf Cubs started.

1917: The movement's headquarters were established in Buckingham Palace Road.

1918: Lady Baden-Powell elected Chief Guide.

1920: Lord Baden-Powell acclaimed Chief Scout of the World.

Glancing back briefly to those early days in Otley when in 1909 three separate patrols were formed by Joe Fieldhouse in the Bridge Avenue area, Eric Cowling in Gay Lane and Tom Dawson in Clapgate.

Scouting gets established

In 1910 they combined under Jim Stead, a veteran of the Boer War, to form a troop – 1st Otley – with its H.Q. in the Three Horseshoes Yard. Later they moved to Bullock Fold in Kirkgate. Another company of lads was formed by the Rev. Granville Biggs 'The Church Lads' Brigade' in 1910. This met with little success due to the attraction of scouting so it changed to a Scout troop – 2nd Otley – with H.Q. in Station Road. The new group was led by the Rev. Biggs with Owen Holmes as assistant, and the griffin motif on the 2nd Otley neckerchief today goes back to those early days and was taken from the Granville Biggs family crest.

In 1913 it was officially registered and the certificate of registration, which the group still possesses, is one of only four early certificates known to exist in the whole movement. The 1st Otley moved their HQ to Wesley Street in 1914, the scoutmaster in this period being Charles Biggs. Later, yet another move to H.Q. in the Methodist Church under Scoutmaster PW Sergeant and assisted by Alan Wright.

The First World War years

The 2nd Otley was kept going during the war by Connie Holmes. When the war ended a Wolf Cub pack was formed in 1918 and its Rover Crew in 1919. The effect of the war and other factors unfortunately caused the 1st Otley to disband in 1923 but many of the Scouts were able to join the 2nd Otley. The spirit of Scouting had not died at the Methodist Church and in 1925 the Otley Methodist troop was formed. Its leaders were Alan Wright and PW Sergeant. This time it was more successful, a Cub Pack and a Rover Crew were formed in 1930. The group is still in existence today. Alan Wright who was Scoutmaster for 40 years was awarded Scouting's highest award the Silver Acorn. 1930 saw the formation of the Parish troop under the leadership of GL Fearnley and assisted by his wife. He will be known to many older members of the town for his newspaper articles under his pen name of 'Silver Fox'. The headquarters at that time were in the old Musgrave Memorial School on Burras Lane.

The Second World War and beyond

The 1939-45 War came along and most troops lost their senior members to war service. The 2nd Otley and Parish troops now shared HQ in the old hut in Burras Lane with patrol leaders in charge. In 1945 Leslie Delderfield joined the Parish Scouts from 2nd Otley as assistant. The victory celebrations were given a traditional send-off with all the Scouts of the town carrying the Sam Ives torch up the Chevin to light the Beacon fire. Rovers of the 2nd Otley set about establishing a 'Den' in Leeds Road, due to the big revival in Scouting after the war. Senior Scouts started nationally in 1948. With this demand the Salem troop at Bridge Church became successful. The Scoutmaster was Arnold Thornton and the troop continues today. 1954 saw the legendary Owen Holmes brother of Connie receive a Silver Acorn. He retired in 1967 having given the Scout movement and 2nd Otley 60 years' service from scouting earliest years. Leslie Delderfield was made an honorary GSL as a very high honour by the Parish troop.

The Advance Party report on Scouting came out in 1967 which has been the basis for change that has kept Scouting abreast of the times. Such changes as 'Boy Scouts' becoming 'Scouts', the introduction of uniform berets and slacks. Most importantly however, the whole training scheme was revised (which was reviewed again in 1977 and in 1999). In 1972 the Parish group expanded to three Cub Packs and in the same year the Chippendale Venture Unit was formed, which catered for young people of over 16 years. Its first leader was Geoff Glen and one of its tasks was the renovation of the old 2nd Otley Rover HQ in Leeds Road which was left when 2nd Otley moved to its new HQ in Craven Street in 1976.

Scouting in Otley since 1977

At the time of the Queen's Silver Jubilee the Mayor of Otley, Councillor Richard Good was prominent in local Scouting with his wife Sheila, and Scouts played a noticeable part in the celebrations. Mr and Mrs Good were leaders at 2nd Otley and throughout the eighties they, and a strong team of adults, ensured that the Group prospered. The 2nd

Otley's fortunes declined for a while but, by 2000, new leaders had revived the group in time for its ninetieth birthday in 2003. Otley Parish enlarged the group headquarters in Burras Lane in stages thanks in part to its enterprising Christmas Post, which it has operated in Otley and district for around the last thirteen years. In the 1980s it linked up with a Scout Group in Arizona and boys from Otley exchanged places with their American counterparts. Its record of producing Queen's Scouts, holders of the highest award in Scouting for young people, is a proud one.

The Otley Bridge Church group have also prospered in spite of a disastrous fire in 1993 which burned down the URC church hall and destroyed all their camping and other equipment. The Group was among the first to welcome girls into its activities when this became national policy in the 1980s. The Otley Methodist group has had a successful period with many camps, but suffering like other organisations from a shortage of adult Leaders from time to time. The deaths of its long-serving Leader Alan Pullan in 2002, who had been a continuous member of Scouting since the age of 8 and a Leader for 41 years, and former Scout leader Les Wilkinson were sad blows. Two County camps were held locally, Chevin '82 catered for over a thousand Scouts from West Yorkshire and in 1991 Weston Venture was another large event held at Weston Park where many outdoor activities were arranged.

Changing with the times

Beaver Scouts originally started in Northern Ireland and spread quickly to cater for 6 to 8 year-olds and the first 'Colony' in Otley was established by Sue Sutcliffe at 2nd Otley in 1986. Very soon the three other local Scout Groups had followed suit. Nationally there were many changes taking place in Scouting such as the ending of headgear and modifications in the uniform. The new training programmes introduced in 1967 were brought up to date in 1985 and by the new millennium changes were afoot again in the shape of new uniforms and programmes which are currently being implemented. The Venture Scout section is being replaced by Explorer Scouts for 14 year-olds and upwards.

Another sign of the times is that some of the Cub and Scout badges for proficiency in activities such as cooking and do-it-yourself are now sponsored by commercial companies such as Macdonalds and B&Q! Members of the Scout groups in Wharfedale have been lucky to have benefited from the help of an active service team composed of present and former leaders and known as the 'Lionhearts'. These stalwarts arrange events for the various sections, such as Cub Sports, a Cub Quiz and a Beaver 'Fun Day' and were instrumental in turning the District campsite at Curly Hill, Ilkley into a well-equipped camping venue. Others played a prominent part in helping the fledgling Otley Carnival to get off the ground at its outset.

Throughout the years since 1977 many people have contributed to the development of Scouting in Otley. The Silver Acorn is the highest award for services to the movement and in this period this honour has been awarded to Sheila Good, Alan Somerton and the late Alan Pullan.

Guiding

Guiding came to Otley in 1920. The 1st Otley Guide Company was formed under the leadership of Mrs Wolffe, with Cathy Moss as assistant. In 1924 Cathy took over leadership and later transferred the company to the Methodist Church, officially registered at Guide Headquarters in London in 1927 as the 2nd Otley Guide Company - the 1st Guide Company then lapsed. In 1931 the 3rd Otley Guide Company was formed at the Parish Church under the leadership of Miss Seaton. Later the same year a Brownie Pack was formed at the Parish Church - this was followed in the 1930's by a Ranger Company with Daisy Booth as Captain.

The Guides came into their own during the war years, helping in a variety of ways with National Service. They helped with children who had been evacuated to the area; several of the Rangers became auxiliary nurses at the hospital at Newall and also at Farnley Hall, which was a Maternity Home during the war. The girls knitted and mended socks for the forces and they 'adopted' a ship; they also entertained patients at the hospital at Christmas time. Some Rangers became fire-watchers. In 1944 the 2nd Otley Brownies were formed at the Methodist Church.

Guiding flourished after the war and in September 1954 the 1st Otley Guide Company was reformed at the Congregational Church. This was followed in 1960 by the opening of the 1st Otley Brownie Pack with Lois Richardson (now Barltrop) in charge.

In 1961 the World Chief Guide visited Headingley and local Guides went to see Lady Baden Powell

In 1968 the Guides helped the mass X-Ray Unit by delivering over 1,700 leaflets to houses all over the town. Later that year 3rd Otley Rangers were reformed.

1970 was the diamond jubilee of the Girl Guide Movement and Otley units attended a County gathering in Harrogate In Otley itself, a special flower bed was displayed in Wharfemeadows Park. An Otley Guide was chosen to represent the District at the Guides' Jubilee Thanksgiving Service in Westminster Abbey in May 1970.

With increased housing developments north of the river, 4th Otley (Parish Church) Brownies were formed at Newall Church Hall in 1971.Also that year an Otley Guide attended the 'White Rose International Camp' held at Robin Hole, where guides from Denmark, Norway, Iceland, Holland and England all camped together. One of the Danish guides then spent a week in Otley.

1972 saw a further growth of the movement in Otley. The 5th Otley (Methodist Church) Brownies, the 6th Otley (Bridge Church) Brownies and 4th Otley Guides were started.

In 1973, one of the District's longest serving Brown Owls - Claire Mountain - retired from 3rd Otley Brownies - but not for long, as she was appointed District Assistant in 1974.

In November 1974, Guiding in Otley suffered a sad loss with the death of Betty Parker aged only 41 years. She had been an inspiration, having been a Brownie, a Guide, an Assistant Girl Guider, and later forming her own Company. Her name is remembered with affection - Guides and Brownies competed annually for two shields 'The Betty Parker Awards' - which were donated to the District by her family. In 1975 The Caley District Ranger Unit was formed.

Jubilee year 1977 saw the formation of 7th Otley Brownie pack at Weston Estate Family Church.

1980 saw Sharon Weston (5th Otley Brownies) being awarded the Star of Merit for courage and fortitude.

In 1982 Otley Guider, Mrs Dorothy Lazarus, was appointed as County Commissioner for the whole of Leeds County.

In November 1985, Otley Guider Tricia Lazarus spent a fortnight in Cuba and Mexico. She was one of two (the other being from Hertfordshire) selected to represent the Guide Association in honour of the 75th anniversary celebrations.

1987 brought the start of Rainbow Guides (5-7 year olds) and 1st Caley Rainbows started not long afterwards.

In 1992, Mrs Lois Barltrop (1st Otley Brownies) was awarded the Star of Merit for courage and fortitude.

In February 1993, 2nd Caley Rainbows were established.

Due to the lack of leaders, 1st and 6th Otley Brownies amalgamated in 1994 - 4th Otley Brownies and Guides closed.

In 1995, Mrs Margaret Frankland became the Division Commissioner for Otley and Guiseley.

Opposite: Bridge Street today. Answer to question on page 17 is, of course, Bridge Street!

1996 brought about the sad death of Guiseley Guider Mrs Angela Nightingale, who had previously been Division Commissioner. She was part of the County Singing Circle and had been in Guiding for very many years.

In 1997, 2nd and 5th Otley Brownies amalgamated. Sadly, in November 1997, Mrs Norma Hunter from 2nd Otley Guides died.

In June 2000, a Fun Day was held at Roundhay Park. This involved Rainbows, Brownies, Guides and Rangers from all over Leeds County. Otley was well represented and an excellent day was had by all. Pool Brownies closed in 2000, along with 3rd Otley (Parish) Brownies (which happily reopened again in the summer of 2001 under new leadership).

In October 2001, Mrs Lois Barltrop received her award for 40 years' service to Guiding at a special service held at the United Reformed Church. In November of that year three performances of 'A Guide Odyssey 2001' were given at a Leeds school involving units from all over Leeds County. Two 2nd Otley Guides took part in the Chevin Division performances, which had a European flavour.

2002 will see many changes in Guiding. Not only have we lost our President with the sad death of Princess Margaret, but we are going to lose some of our most loved and respected leaders when they retire in the summer - Mrs Lois Barltrop (41 years' service), Mrs Jean Jackson (14 years' service) and Mrs Sylvia King (33 years' service).

Otley now has two Rainbow Units, five Brownie Packs and three Guide Units.

Service Organisations

Rotary Club of Otley

Formed in 1933 to encourage the ideal of service by the individual in personal, business and community life. Rotarians are professional businessmen and women who work as volunteers to improve the quality of life in their local community and internationally. Rotary clubs meet weekly, are non-political, non-religious and open to all cultures, races and creeds. 'Service above Self' is the motto of Rotary which is the largest charity in the world. The Rotary Club of Otley supports and gives financial help to local charities and to young people undertaking international social work, as well as aiding local schools with special projects. On an international level, Rotary has raised money to help eradicate polio throughout the world.

Otley Lions Club

Founded 1980 as part of Lions Club International. Its mission is 'to create and foster a spirit of understanding among all people for humanitarian needs by providing voluntary services through community involvement and international cooperation'.

Through the years the Lions have raised a huge amount of money by various means, many readers will have given their old books to the Lions' collection for example. Their efforts are mostly local but others involving clubs in Yorkshire have raised approximately £70,000. Much of this has been to support local community groups and major world appeals. Members, thank you for your support.

Royal British Legion

British Legion formed 21st April 1925 and Royal British Legion 10th September 1971.

The Legion aims to relieve need and to further the education of beneficiaries and their spouses, children and dependants. Beneficiaries being any person who has served in the Royal Navy, Royal Air Force or Army, and some Auxiliary services. The Legion is responsible for running the poppy appeal, maintaining and servicing several convalescent homes, assisting financially many widows of ex service persons, and running educational facilities to help ex service personnel when they retire from service.

The high point is the Remembrance Day Parade held near to the 11th day of the 11th month. Parades are organised by branches worldwide, and there is a Festival of Remembrance at the Royal Albert Hall in London.

St John Ambulance

Formed in 1901 to teach first aid and related subjects to adults and youth members, and to provide first aid cover for local events. Otley branch provides cover at Otley Show, Otley Carnival, local theatres and athletic events.

Since 1986 the members have used a purpose built headquarters on Myerscroft. In 2001 the Group celebrated its centenary with a weekend away at West End Outdoor Centre, attended by past and present members. A certificate was presented by the County Commander to commemorate the event.

Women's Royal Voluntary Service

Formed by Lady Reading as a wartime measure as the Women's Voluntary Service, and in later years given royal approval, hence WRVS. The WRVS in partnership with public and private sectors, aims to be a premier provider of voluntary assistance to those in need of care within their communities.

Otley WRVS has provided a tea bar at Wharfedale Hospital for over 30 years, and members also take a daily newspaper trolley round the wards. Meals on wheels have been delivered by volunteers to people in Otley and Pool in Wharfedale for many years. They also help at local events. There is an emergency team trained to help in any emergency or crisis that can be called out by the police, social services and the fire brigade. The emergency team served refreshments daily to the police and armed services at the Dunkeswick air crash in 1995. They have also staffed teams during flooding and helped when the Kosovo refugees came to Otley hospital.

Otley Women's Institute

Formed in 1984, the WI provides social and educational opportunities for women from the age of 16, and gives them an opportunity to express their opinions on matters of interest to the whole nation. Monthly meetings with visiting speakers are held in Otley Civic Centre, and an annual coffee morning and a Victorian Fayre Stall raises money for local charities. Through county and national federations of institutes WI members vote annually on National Resolutions about matters of concern, for example, the funding of children's hospices, which are then taken up with Her Majesty's Government.

Otley Ladies Hospital Group

Formed in 1950 to mobilise, encourage, foster and maintain the interest of the public in patients, and to support the work of the Wharfedale Hospital. The group holds an annual garden party to raise funds for any items of equipment which will benefit patients of the hospital. Two members visit patients each week and the visits are much appreciated. Each Christmas, patients receive a gift.

Otley Townswomen's Guild

Formed in 1938 to inform and educate women in a mutually supportive organisation, and to influence the Government on matters appertaining to women, the Guild raises funds for local charities including Otley Action for Older People, Multiple Sclerosis and the Beamsley Project. Monthly meetings are held on the first Tuesday (except August) in the Civic Centre with visiting speakers, Special interest groups include: readers, recreation, fabric craft, choir, and art. A Buttercross stall is held every year. A wall hanging in the Civic Centre worked by members of Otley Townswomen's Guild celebrates 60 years of the Guild.

Freemasons

Freemasonry in Otley was established in 1866 when the Wharfedale Lodge was consecrated by the Rt. Hon. the Earl of De Grey and Ripon. Meetings were held at the Fleece Inn in Westgate until 1876 and then transferred to the Masonic Hall in Boroughgate. In 1937 the Harewood Lodge was visited by HRH Prince Arthur, Duke of Connaught, the third son of Queen Victoria who gave permission for the title to be changed to Royal Wharfedale Lodge.

Due to cramped accommodation at Boroughgate the lodges moved to Westbourne House previously the family home of Colin Greenwood an Otley solicitor The lodges have met there since 1968 and have been joined by three Leeds Lodges. Freemasonry

Opposite: Brian Barker and Jess Lee could split a hide to an accuracy of 0·1mm on a band knife.

offers its members an approach to life which seeks to reinforce thoughtfulness for others, kindness in the community, honesty in business, courtesy in society and fairness in all things. It also teaches and practises concern for people, care of the less fortunate and help for those in need. For example Otley Freemasons have recently provided football strips for a needy local junior team and have made a donation towards the rebuilding of the sports clubhouse recently burnt down. Money for deserving causes comes from members' pockets. Larger sums are given nationally for medical research, helping the aged and annual payments to hospices throughout the country, to name but a few.

Tanning

Tanning and skinning were the principal industries in the town up to the mid- nineteenth century, and the earliest recorded reference to tanning is in the document known as 'The Extent of Otley', and the entry – 'Juliana le Barker, free tenant, owns 1 acres and meadow.' A tanner was one who prepared the leather, and the name in the middle ages was barker, from the bark of oak trees used in the process.

Between 1600 – 1800, a family named Flesher were the principal tanners with a tannery in Crow Lane, and some readers may remember a small row of cottages (pulled down in 1964), the rear yards being entered under a stone arch which bore the initials 'T F 1767' This property backed on to Paradise Square, known earlier as Tanners Fold and now a car park.

At the beginning of the last century, Robert Barker was the principal tanner and fell-monger, owning a tan-yard and bark mill in what is now Station Road. Others in the town were Horsman (Boroughgate), Denbigh (later Lawson) and Young (previously Flesher) in Crow Lane.

Robert Barker appears to have relinquished tanning in 1850, but continued the leather dressing business in the Cross Green premises (previously Forsters) and William Lawson took over the Barker tan-pits in Station Road.

The Cross Green factory was enlarged by William, son of Robert Barker, who also built a factory in Gay Lane (as a currier), but the latter was later sold to H Lund in 1931. In 1902 the firm was described as Curriers and Levant Dressers, and in 1905 made a limited company, with W H, Robert, Thomas W, Norman L, A S and P R Barker as directors.

Having outlived the other tanners and curriers businesses, this old established firm could claim a continuity from Robert Barker to its last controllers, Mr W H and Mr B D Barker (sons of Thomas W Barker) in the late 1980s. They dressed hides and tanned English sheepskins, for leather handbags and fancy leather goods in markets as far afield as Warsaw and America.

However, things were to change drastically. The supply of Indian hides, which were the basic raw material for Barkers because of their thin profile compared with native hides, came to an end as India developed the skills and equipment to process its own hides.

Fortunately for the Barker Brothers, retirement was just a short time away. They closed the tannery and sold its equipment. In May 1989, within a week of having sold the tannery, it was subject to arson. The buildings valued at £300,000 were reduced to a burnt out shell despite the efforts of fire-fighting appliances from fourteen surrounding stations.

Thereafter, the buildings were demolished and the site re-developed as housing.

Did Northgate come this way?

Historical References

Otley Museum

Otley Museum is housed in the Civic Centre building, Cross Green, formerly the Mechanics Institute.

It is a local history museum with a large documentary collection and a range of exhibits reflecting the social and industrial history of Otley from prehistoric times to the twenty-first century.

Specialist collections include a large archive devoted to the history of Otley's printing machine industry, which developed from the invention of the famous 'Wharfedale' machine in the town by William Dawson and David Payne. The Eric Cowling flint collection is an indication of Otley's significance as a prehistoric settlement.

Otley Museum is recognised as a Registered Museum under the auspices of the Council for Museums Archives and Libraries and is run as a charitable trust, entirely self-funded with the help of its 'Friends' scheme and staffed by volunteers who aim to give all types of visitors friendly and individual attention whilst conserving the exhibits and documents to a high standard for the promotion of public interest and education. We welcome local people and those from further afield including researchers, university students and schoolchildren.

The management committee believe that the maintenance of this significant collection is an important part of preserving the individual character of Otley and hope to continue to develop this great potential.

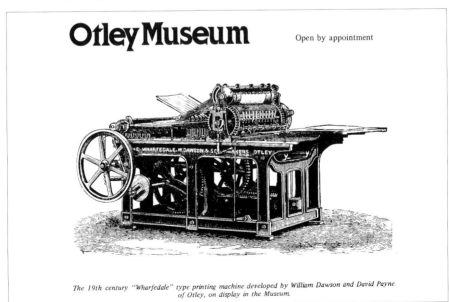

Otley Museum   Open by appointment

The 19th century "Wharfedale" type printing machine developed by William Dawson and David Payne of Otley, on display in the Museum.

Thomas Chippendale

In the year 1718 one of Otley's most famous sons, Thomas, was born to Mary and John Chippendale. His baptism is recorded in the Parish register of 5 June 5th 1718. His father was a local 'joyner' and the family is reputed to have lived at one time on the present site of the Skipton Building Society in Boroughgate. Young Thomas learnt the art of working with oak, ash, elm and lime from both his father and his Uncle Joseph. When his mother died he lived with his uncle and when he was ready he left for London, to seek fame and fortune.

We can trace his movements from Long Acre to St. Martins Lane and it is from here that he published 'The Gentleman and Cabinet Maker's Director'. This made him a household name, subsequently giving him commissions to make fine furniture for many of England's grandest houses, such as Harewood, Nostell Priory, Denton, etc. Pieces of furniture from these houses are now in the ownership of the Society.

He became a member of the Society of Arts in 1760. Thomas died in 1779 and is buried at St. Martins, London.

The Chippendale Society was founded in Otley by the late Mr. Tom Pickles who also published a book on the life of Thomas Chippendale. The Society's aims are to keep Chippendale furniture in Britain and if possible in the houses for which it was originally made. The Society hold a dinner each year on or near Thomas Chippendale's baptismal date of 5 June and has produced a colour plated catalogue of its collection. This publication is on sale at the Otley Museum and copies can also be obtained from the Secretary. It is now planned to establish a web site which it is hoped will be up and running soon. The Chippendale ride through the Danefield Estate has been lined with trees donated by over 100 people, the first in the ride being a lime tree presented by Her Majesty Queen Elizabeth II.

The Ron Kitching Library

Located in the rebuilt and refurbished premises of Otley Cycling Club is a unique collection built up over a period of more than 60 years by the dedication of Ron Kitching, champion cyclist and businessman. Here are bound copies of cycling magazines, club magazines, photographs, biographies, unique cycling drawings and cartoons and a host of items going back over 100 years that will appeal to all cyclists.

Otley Audio Archive

An on-going project begun coincidentally with Jubilee year by John Morgan and funded by a Lottery Millennium Award. It is a series of recordings, capturing the memories, experiences and observations of people, both old and young, from long ago or more recently. These cherished memories inform, entertain and enlighten and help to ensure our history is not lost for future generations.

Major Sports Clubs

Otley Cricket Club

Otley Cricket Club was formed on 1820 but that's not to say there wasn't cricket in the town before that. There was willow, there were balls, patches of grass and young men ... so there must have been cricket! There's been cricket on Cross Green since 1862, but until Otley joined the Wharfedale and Airedale League in 1893 there were only 'friendlies'. Even with league status, matches could have hardly been hostile: there was underarm bowling only and no boundaries.

Otley's first professional was a gentleman from Sheffield called Luke Reaney. He was signed in April 1875; had to be on duty every day except Sunday from 2pm to dusk, and earned £2 2s a week. In the 1870s, Otley's Ted Wilkinson took five wickets in five balls against Rotherham. In 1906 Mr F 'Wharfedale Catapult' Swainston took eight wickets for six runs against Ilkley. A history stretching back 157 years ... but as if to prove the Club's as good as ever, Otley won the League in 1974 and the Cup in 1976. Since 1977 Otley CC had a great run of success until the 1996 season when the team was ageing and began a poor run of results. Prior to 1996 the Club were League Champions seven times, Waddilove Cup Winners five times and finalists in the Yorkshire Champions Trophy twice. The Second XI were League Champions twice and Birtwhistle Cup Winners twice as well as the club winning the Burmah Oil Trophy on three occasions. There is a thriving Junior Section with coaching at Cross Green. The last two years have seen a revival in the fortunes of Otley CC and the Club has great hopes of challenging for promotion back to the top division this year.

Old Otliensians Rugby Club

Following an informal discussion in 1925 by rugby-minded old scholars of Prince Henry's Grammar School, the Club was formed the following year and several games were played in 1926/27. Among those involved in the early years were Fred and Bill Greetham and Arthur Kitching.

The war brought a halt to what had developed into a successful junior Club. However, in 1947, mainly through the efforts of Ron Mountain, the first post-war Secretary, the Club became firmly re-established and in 1948/49, two strong teams were again fielded using school facilities. Others involved in the re-formation of the Club included Hereward Brown, Jack Crossley, Geoffrey Storr and Ernest Wardman.

The Club continued to make good progress and this was highlighted by the winning of the Yorkshire Shield in the 1958/59 season against Castleford. In 1966, following efforts by the President, the late Mr N Bousefield, and the Secretary, the late Mr T A Chaffer (after whom the ground is named), a lease on the present land off Pool Road was obtained. Initially, changing rooms and kitchen facilities were provided and the ground was eventually purchased in 1972. The clubroom and bar were opened the following year, coinciding with the closure of the Club's former headquarters at the White Horse Hotel in Manor Square.

The Club continued to prosper throughout the '70s running four senior sides and a Colts. In the 1980/81 season they reached the Yorkshire Silver Trophy final and when Leagues were first introduced in the 1987/88 season, they gained steady promotion into what was then Yorkshire League 1. In 1993 a stylish and welcoming new clubroom and bar were opened and the playing areas continue to be the envy of clubs throughout Yorkshire.

Since the Club was re-formed in the late forties, Hon. Life Members Noel Fortune, George Leach and Geoff Storr have been actively involved in the running of the Club. Among other duties, Noel was Team Secretary for twenty-eight years and continued playing regularly well into his late fifties.

The Club is still thriving, having won the Aire-Wharfe Cup last season and being a strong promotion contender in Yorkshire League 3 this season. For the future, 'Ensians are looking at the development of new changing facilities and floodlights, whilst building on links with hockey and other sports may feature in longer-term plans.

Angling

First records of an angling club go back to 1873.

The first minuted meeting was in 1876 with a membership of 30 paying subscriptions of £2 per annum. 1901 saw temporary closure of the club due to heavy water pollution. June 1907 saw a revived club which has continued to the present day with a membership of 200. The club re-stocks the river annually with some 4,000 trout. The activities of the club are restricted to Otley residents and the fishing is reserved as a trout water.

Opposite: The river Wharfe when we used to get a real winters!

Jimmy Nettleton, a saddler of Otley, together with a selected few members would be asked, when the Duke of Devonshire was entertaining Royalty, to fish the Wharfe at Bolton Abbey to supply the breakfast table. Their reward was any fish caught over 1lb. The summer of 2000 saw the establishment of new fishing ponds at Knotford Nook designed for use by disabled anglers, the funding coming from the Millennium Festival Awards, Otley Social Club and a club charity match.

Otley Swimming Club

Otley Swimming Club, formed in 1903 by a group of local gentlemen, originally held its training sessions in the waters of the river Wharfe, before relocating to the nearby open-air swimming pool in Wharfemeadows Park. Over the years, thousands of local children have been taught to swim at the club.

Many notable feats were achieved by swimmers guided by the Otley Swimming Club coaches. Amongst these, Barry Watson swam the Channel in record time in 1965, while in 1969 Kendall Mellor became the first to swim the 26 miles from Minorca to Majorca.

The club moved into the newly built indoor pool, at Prince Henry's Grammar School, in the early 70s, and continued to produce top class swimmers from county to international standard. The most recent of these were Elena Arter, who went on to represent her country, and elite triathlete Richard Allen, who just missed out on selection for the 2000 Sydney Olympics.

The club has organised many trips abroad, to Ireland, and also to France, for exchange visits with the swimmers from Otley's twin town of Montereau. These trips have not been possible in recent years, due to a falling membership. Neglect of the pool facilities

over the years by Leeds City Council, has been mirrored by a decline in the fortunes of the club. Breakdowns of the boiler system and filtration plant led to many chilly swim sessions and more than a few cancellations. The team of volunteers that runs the committee and carries out the teaching/coaching duties, has strived to keep the club afloat against the odds. Hopefully, its perseverance will be rewarded following the recent £350k refurbishment, completed at the end of March, following a six month closure.

Otley Cycle Club

Otley Cycle Club has a thriving and active community with over 120 members. Formed on 27 January 1927, having started life as the Otley Road Club nearly 100 years ago, the club now has a well fitted out club house in Crow Lane (Wellcroft House), and a host of activities throughout the year

The club organises time trials over various distances from 10 to 100 miles and a marathon 12 hour event whilst club riders regularly challenge for top honours in a range of national and regional events. The local time trial is run around the 'Pool Triangle' on most Thursday evenings throughout the summer months. For the leisure cyclist the club organises a series of club runs starting at 9 am from the Buttercross on Sundays throughout the year with 7.30pm Wednesday evening rides throughout the summer months (May – September). Suited to riders of all abilities these take the cyclist through some of the best scenery in Yorkshire with regular tea and coffee stops along the way.

To celebrate the Queen's Jubilee, the Club is organising a 75 mile and 75km cycle ride on 4 June 2002 with all riders completing the circuit receiving a souvenir of the occasion.

Changes in Cycling

There have been massive changes in the past 25 years. The heyday of cycling, mainly road cycling in the 30s was followed by a dramatic fall in the late 50s. Then along came the BMX bike closely followed by the mountain bike. The latter has developed into traditional cross country, downhill and trials; bikes being developed for the different disciplines. Suspension bikes owe much of their performance and design to the aero industry.

Cycling today has many sub-divisions all enjoying great popularity and people are once again on two wheels. Chevin Cycles that was once a small 'roadies' shop in Gay Lane has become one of the premier shops in the north of England in its new premises.

Otley Golf Club

In September 1906 a meeting was called in the Mechanics Institute to investigate the founding of a Golf Club. A committee was formed under the presidency of Mr F Horton-Fawkes. Mr F Waite, the first Captain of the Club, was a founder member. His trophy is still played for today.

The first one hundred members paid a subscription of 2 guineas (£2.10) and within a month they had acquired the lease of some land off Bradford Road. The course was laid out later that year by H Fulford and H Loveridge, a clubhouse was erected on Bradford

Road and the official opening was held in 1907. A greenkeeper was retained for 28s a week (£1.40) and the rules were drawn up for competitions, some of which are still held today.

The current members continue to bless their forefathers for the foresight displayed in 1913 when the land was purchased. In 1965 the building of the present clubhouse in the centre of the land necessitated the course being re-arranged. Further land has since been bought to cope with the demands of a membership of some 700 people, and a policy of encouraging and promoting ladies and junior members.

Otley Sailing Club

The club was founded in 1958 by a group of local businessmen who were interested in sailing on a Wednesday early evening. In those days shops were closed for a half day every week, and the opportunity to go sailing was too good to resist. Dinghy sailing as we know it today, was in its infancy with boats being developed by people like Jack Holt and Uffar Fox. Some of their designs are still sailed at Weston Water today: Enterprise, Graduate, GP14, and Mirror.

The club developed and expanded with the help and support of Tilcon who owned the gravel pits at Knotford Nook. The sailing extended to Sundays and the season lengthened: instead of finishing in early October it ran from early March to New Year's Day. Competitive sailing was introduced and Otley was represented successfully at local, national, and international regattas. In 1977 Tilcon sold the gravel pit to a local developer and the sailing club was forced to look for a new home. Fortunately ARC, a rival sand and gravel company, was developing workings at the opposite end of Otley and wanted to show its willingness to support local people and sport. In the autumn of 1997 the sailing club moved from the east to the west of Otley. The strip of water available at the new site seemed very small after the old lake but promises from ARC of the things to come helped to encourage members to expand and develop the facilities at the site. A road three quarters of a mile long was laid by hand. With the help of funding from the Sports Council, the members built a permanent clubhouse complete with changing rooms and facilities for disabled sailors. Over the past 20 years the club has led the way in promoting a sport for all minority groups within the sailing world. It has taught a young lady blind from birth to sail single-handed and encouraged groups of children with severe learning difficulties to sail. The club works closely with Prince Henry's School and John Smeaton School in Leeds providing sailing lessons to pupils free of charge. The club is looking forward to its silver jubilee and hopes to continue providing a first class sailing venue in the area for many years to come.

Otley Town Sports and Social Club

Formed by an amalgamation of Otley AFC and Dawson Payne & Elliott football clubs in 1972, Otley Town Sports and Social Club was then joined by Grove Hill Cricket Club and in 1999 by Otley Express Junior Football Club.

The original clubhouse buildings consisted of the garage and the present changing facilities. After amalgamation, the 'shed' was brought down from DP&E, attached to the building and is now the main clubroom. The cricket section joined the Leeds and District League. Generous funding from local businessman Mick Davies built a scoreboard in 1984. The clubhouse was refurbished in 1988, to include the Jim Wallace Lounge, named in the memory of the club's late President. Jim had been Chairman of Otley AFC in 1952 and his wife Marjorie was Secretary. Derek Hawley joined Grove Hill in the mid 50s succeeding Jim as President. The clubhouse is being refurbished in 2002 with a new bar area, kitchen and toilets.

The Old Show Ground has hosted many cricket and football finals. Not many clubs can say that they have hosted a British Cup Final. In the 70's, Leeds played Glasgow in the final of the British Deaf Cup at the Old Show Ground and Otley referee, Keith Urquhart, realising his whistle was of no use used a big handkerchief instead.

Otley Town organises one of the most successful six-a-side tournaments in the area, with teams coming from Hull, Lancashire and South Yorkshire.

Little is known about the beginnings of Otley AFC, but limited records show the club was originally formed as Otley Parish Church shortly after the First World War. It was renamed Otley AFC towards the end of the Second World War with local players, soldiers from the local camp and a few German prisoners of war making up the team. After the war, players changed in a pub on Kirkgate and played at Garnetts field. The club also played at Wharfemeadows for a time. After a game the players used to bathe in an old tin bath in the back yard of the pub.

When Otley Show moved from the Old Show Field in Pool Road, Otley AFC saw the opportunity and made it into their home ground.

The popular Workshops competition took place at the end of each season, involving local works teams, including Garnetts, the Wharfedale, Sinclairs, DP&E, Weegmans and the Three Horse Shoes.

Many people have been involved with Otley AFC since the war, but special mention must go to 'bag man' Eric Paley, Chairman Jim Wallace, and leading goalscorer Stuart Dyson who scored over 260 goals from 1954-1961.

Dawson Payne & Elliott/Crabtree Mann (now Safeways)

Dawson Payne and Elliott owned a cricket and football pitch on the opposite side of their works in Burras Lane. When the site was sold, the team played their games at Wharfeside and the Grammar School fields. In 1972, the team amalgamated with Otley AFC. Dawson Payne and Elliott started life in the Wharfedale League and went on to play in the West Yorkshire League. Club stalwarts, Dennis Blackburn, Alan McGee, Dr John Metcalf and Norman Cockerham, saw the club through from its early years to become part of the present day set-up. Some players went on to, or had played at, a professional level.

Otley Town AFC

After the amalgamation of Otley AFC and DP&E, the new football team, Otley Town, played in the West Yorkshire League. Otley Town now runs three senior teams. Former first team captain, Peter Atkinson, went on to play for Guiseley and twice played at Wembley for them in the final of the FA Trophy.

Grove Hill Cricket Club

Grove Hill CC began life as Otley Mills Cricket Club in 1922, originally for employees of the nearby mill. It played in the grounds of Grove Hill House on Ilkley Road. The property belonged to the Duncan family. Otley Council purchased Grove Hill Park in 1968 and the team became known as Grove Hill CC. Amalgamation with Otley Town took place in 1974 and the lengthy process of laying a wicket on the Old Show Ground took place. In 1977, the club finally moved down Pool Road. In 1980 now as Otley Town CC the club joined the Leeds and District League after 24 seasons with the Dales Council in which 24 trophies had been won.

Cricket at Otley Town had survived on the loyalty of a number of members over the years and with the retirement of long time club stalwarts, Stan Handford and in recent years Derek and Maureen Hawley, the section went downhill quickly and disbanded at the end of the 1998-99 season.

Otley Express

In 1978, Otley All Saints Middle School organised a successful trip to America for the school football team. On return the organising teacher, Peter Jones, kept the boys together and, using an American style name, started Otley Express. Brian Fawell, stalwart of Otley Town, saw his son play in the first ever Otley Express team. As the age groups expanded, several pitches were used around the town. Eventually in the late nineties, Express amalgamated with Otley Town Sports and Social Club.

Spurred on by the new edition of this book, Keith Urquhart has produced a lengthy history of Cricket and Football in Otley.

Otley's Missing Sports Centre

Otley Sports Council campaigned over 15 years to get a sports centre but, despite many meetings, promises made were broken. Leeds City Council did eventually apply for a Lottery Grant to upgrade facilities at Prince Henry's Grammar School but this was eventually rejected by Sport England. A large part of the application was for refurbishment and outstanding maintenance work. The final outcome was that Leeds City Council pledged matched funding of £350,000 plus contributions from the Ward Councillors' CIT fund and Prince Henry's Grammar School. This has enabled the tired pool to be renovated, the work being carried out as we prepare this book.

Health Services in Otley 1977-2002

Since the Silver Jubilee in 1977, there have been major changes in every aspect of health care in Otley. Hospital Care, General Practice and Community Services have all seen major changes which are still ongoing.

The building of a brand new state of the art Hospital is about to begin.

Every general practice in the Town has purpose-built premises, computers and many more staff (doctors, nurses and ancillary) to care for patients and develop services. Community Services have also changed and are more responsive to patient needs.

The big mental hospitals (High Royds and Scalebor Park) have gone or about to go.

The tuberculosis (TB) Sanatoria (Middleton and Grassington) have gone.

General Surgeons and General Physicians have been replaced by many more super Specialists who visit the hospital but are based in Leeds.

The GP Out of Hours service is now provided by a co-operative scheme in which all local GP partners participate, providing 24-hour cover in all the Wharfe Valley area, using a vehicle for home visits with life saving equipment, and urgent consultation centres.

The new hospital is the result of over 25 years' campaigning by every section of the local community. Initial success, with a new Maternity Unit, a new ward for older peoples' medicine and major expansion of Out Patients and X-Ray fizzled out in the late 80s. The main wards were past their useful life, and after 15 years of community pressure we are now about to see the results of our efforts.

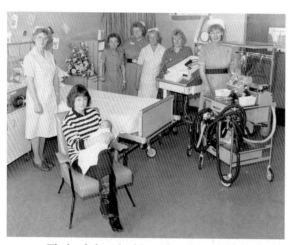

The last baby to be delivered in Otley Hospital

From 1984 in quick succession every general practice in town built new enlarged premises to accommodate the increased range of services. Nurses were employed to keep up immunisation and screening targets, to develop new services and take over some of the services GPs had been doing. For instance, through their efforts in immunisation measles, mumps and rubella, which had been a scourge for generations, virtually disappeared, just as polio had been a scourge in the first half of the Queen's reign and vanished. At the same time every practice developed its computer systems. Expansion has been extremely rapid. Now most prescriptions are computer-generated, many records are held on computer and it is possible to transfer investigation results electronically. GP appointments, still a novelty in the first half of the Queen's reign, are now the norm and are usually booked electronically.

The closure of thousands of hospital beds in elderly care and mental health has resulted in a massive rise in the number of nursing and rest homes. There are many in Otley and the Wharfe Valley.

Hospital management had been very local, starting with the Otley and Ilkley Hospital Management Committee, but this has now been taken over by management from Leeds.

General Practice has changed from the West Riding to Leeds and is now managed by a Primary Care Trust. From very little central bureaucracy, to a major management input. At the time of writing the Trust is less than a month old so it is too early to know if the additional expense will show in better results.

Miscellaneous Services:

Otley and District Talking Newspaper

The aim is to supply on audiotape the news from the local newspaper to the blind, the partially sighted, or to persons who cannot read it for themselves. Derek Hodgson, with a grant from the R.N.I.B, started the newspaper in 1984. He found listeners, purchased a recorder, mixer, microphones, copier, cassettes, and taught volunteers how to use them. He also recruited readers and hired a room and when the grant ran out 52 tapes were being despatched weekly. In 1985 he handed over the task to volunteers who have run it since. Nowadays 120 tapes are sent out, with a magazine in alternate months.

Shopmobility Scooter Hire

A scheme from Otley Town council to enable people with mobility problems to get around Otley. The electric mobility scooters are housed at the Civic Centre and are loaned for two-hour periods.

Otley Action for Older People

Otley Action for Older People aims to promote choice and opportunity with older people in Otley by offering a wide range of activities and services including:
Social Activities: entertainment, trips, outings, and mini day centres for those older people who require support to get out.

Supporting independence at home through gardening, decorating, small-scale maintenance, security equipment and advice and information on household matters.

Individual and personal support: help with transport, home visiting, befriending scheme and a quarterly newsletter.

Otley Matters

A community newsletter funded by the Town Council and compiled by the Community Development Worker. This is delivered to all households four times a year and has a vast coverage of local community groups and organisations that benefit the residents. It also gives information on funding and provides information on how to contact local councillors and MPs. Past special editions have concentrated on the future of Wharfedale Hospital and in April this year The Transport Edition

Conservation

Conservation areas are areas of special architectural or historic interest, the character and appearance of which it is desirable to preserve and enhance. Otley Conservation Area, born of the Civic Amenities Act of 1967, coincides with the site of the town as it stood in the Middle Ages. Its rich and distinctive nature, with that of several adjoining areas of conservation interest, reminds us of our forebears' toil and ingenuity in response to their surroundings and to the unique geographical context of their town. Their resources were hard-won from the landscape. Since ancient times, blocks of stone were hewn from Chevin quarries and hauled to the valley floor where they, with timber and (later) slate, were forged into townscape. Itself now a valuable resource, the product tells the story of Otley like a special sort of book, one which we are learning to read, enabling us to conserve and cultivate our forebears' town properly, for ourselves and future generations to enjoy.

New Inn Court 2002

Since 1977, Otley realised developments that undoubtedly influenced the feel of the town, not least its conservation area. Replacing the railway with a by-pass, building a supermarket where Crabtree Vickers' works stood on Westgate in the 1980s, and continued suburban house-building are examples. They represent a movement away from organic evolution of a market town over centuries to the dull uniformity imposed by modern, anonymous convenience living. We turned our backs on what shaped Otley for the last thousand years and looked to city life for inspiration and, whilst we were distracted, these changes rapidly took place. Even the control of how Otley develops now lies with a city, whose traditions are very different from those of Otley.

It could, however, have been worse. The sidelining of Otley since the 1960s diverted pressures to remodel built heritage elsewhere. We watched places like Sheffield being torn apart to make way for 'progress', and we witnessed concrete, steel and glass replace cherished buildings in Leeds. Having benefited from being spectators, Otley people steadily became more conscious of the high material value of the town's numerous built heritage survivals. Becoming better informed, we learned to question schemes being proposed that would do little to preserve or enhance the Conservation Area and, indeed, areas beyond that are just as worthy of conserving.

Is this conservation?

In Otley Conservation Area (like any other), restoration of a derelict shell is only part of the story. Could the previous use of a building be reinstated? Could another use be found that would contribute to a healthy, sustainable, mixed economy? Could our featureless and untidily maintained tarmac streets once again be paved with setts to complete the living, working scene?

Conservation projects, like revitalisation of the former New Inn Yard in 1987 and the conversion of Otley Liberal Club and Manor House stables in 2001, are bringing life back into the town and ensuring survival of its fine buildings. Recent refurbishment of dilapidated setts in Station Road, Mount Pisgah and Crow Lane is also promising, yet inferior shop front designs continue to disfigure Kirkgate and other key parts of the conservation area.

Otley Town Council, with other groups (many voluntary) and an increasing number of individuals, have it at heart to sustain life and tradition in the town which, if successful, will inherently preserve and enhance Otley Conservation Area, and nurture the power of place.

Environmental Improvements in Otley

To minimise destructive activities on this planet we have to 'think globally but act locally.' That is what some local groups have done, and will continue to do in Otley. They have put thoughts and words into actions that contribute to the sustainability and bio-diversity of the area.

The Gallows Hill Nature Park has been created from the former Otley Sewage Works to the east of Otley. This site adjacent to the River Wharfe which was neglected, overgrown and rubbish-strewn has been transformed into a well-managed area of native tree and shrub planting, grassed areas, walkways and a large wild-life pond. Many species of plants and animals are benefiting. A small car park has been laid out and a dog bin is available for dog owners to use. A bird log is kept by the Friends of Gallows Hill and so far 66 species of birds have been seen in, or flying over, the site. The Friends have met regularly on site since 1996 and are usually there on the first Sunday of each month.

The Kell Beck flows from its source to the North of Otley through farmland and then through a 'green corridor' at the backs of houses and eventually joins the River Wharfe near Otley Bridge. This beck has been monitored for five years or so by the Friends of Kell Beck who aim to ensure that the beck is free-flowing and try to minimise problems at times of flash flooding. Wildflower, shrubs and bulb planting are ongoing projects and the creation of a butterfly garden is under development. There are regular action days which involve collecting litter, and cutting back of overhanging trees and hedges as necessary. Verges adjacent to the path are cut back to allow people to walk past but leave habitats for wildlife. The Friends of Kell Beck, together with many

residents who live alongside the beck, are slowly improving the beck and its immediate surroundings. Kingfishers, bats and butterflies are often seen in the area. An interesting illustrated booklet 'The Kell Beck Walk' describing local history along and near the beck has been published.

Other groups such as the Friends of Well Croft have improved Teal Beck and its surrounding grassed area with a much-modified children's play area with safety in mind. Many other people contribute to enhancing the environment in Otley and the Britain in Bloom Group endeavours to encourage everyone to brighten up their gardens or shop fronts with flowers. Local schools have created wildlife gardens and ponds and encouraged frogs. There are many areas that have benefited in the last few years in Otley but there are still many other neglected pieces of land, allotments and gardens in Otley that could be improved whether it be planting flowers for butterflies, building ponds for frogs, providing boxes for bats or the construction of an energy-efficient and environmentally friendly building.

Natural History

A naturalist living in Otley is fortunate in there being a variety of habitats within easy reach of the town. The focal point is the river which in its shallow parts, especially where it passes Wharfemeadows Park below the weir, has a decidedly highland aspect, affording a suitable habitat for dippers and grey wagtails. Here, too, grows a mass of water buttercups whilst lower downstream the banks are lined with a rich tangle of grasses and umbelliferous plants in the summer. Here where the water is deeper and the flow less rapid, the river takes on more of a lowland aspect and various species of wildfowl can be seen on the water during the winter months. The kingfisher normally nests in the sandy clay banks and so do sand martins. Herons fish the river and during the spring these birds can regularly be seen flying from the river to the small heronry which has become established in recent years in the Washburn Valley.

The flooded gravel pits east of the town are a favourite haunt of bird watchers in the winter when many waterfowl are attracted there. Mostly the species are common enough, coot being particularly abundant. There is usually a resident flock of semi-wild Canada geese. Occasionally rarities put in an appearance and in recent years both Slavonian grebes and smew have been seen. The reservoirs of the Washburn Valley are well known for their wintering population of water birds. For details there are the annual 'Transactions' of the Wharfedale Naturalists Society.

The Washburn Valley is a fine place for studying wildlife as it offers a superbly unspoiled rural area of mixed habitats, the woodlands in particular supporting a good variety of birds, plants and insects. Pied flycatchers, redstarts and wood warblers are the most notable summer visitors to the valley, whilst in winter flocks of immigrant thrushes are a feature, the two most abundant species being fieldfares and redwings. Plants of note include the alternate leafed golden saxifrage and panicled sedge.

The moors north of the town provide the most specialised and unique habitat, with a typical highland fauna and flora. Most conspicuous amongst the plants is the heather but there are others, particularly in boggy places, which are well worth searching for. These include such gems as the bog asphodel, sundew and winter green. Insects associated with the moors include some with a mainly northern distribution in Britain of which the most striking are the beetle carabus nitens and the northern eggar moth whose hairy caterpillars are eaten by cuckoos. The red grouse is abundant on the moors. Other species to be found include the golden plover, curlew and short-eared owl.

Chevin Forest Park

In August 1944 Major Le GGW Horton-Fawkes of Farnley Hall gave 263 acres of land on Otley Chevin to the people of Otley. In a letter to the Otley Urban District Council he said 'Your Council may even now be considering alternative forms of war memorials. It occurs to me that an open space which can be beautified by trees and preserved in a natural state might offer an opportunity as a memorial to all who fought and furthered the war of Freedom on all fronts'. (Source: Wharfedale & Airedale Observer archives.)

Areas of land on the Chevin had been in the ownership of the Fawkes family since before 1290 when it was mentioned as belonging to John Fawkes, then King's Steward of the Forest of Knaresborough. An 1896 Game Book entry from Farnley Hall records the numbers of rabbits, hare, pheasant and partridges shot on the Caley Beat.

In 1803 during the threat of French invasion, the Chevin was one of the chosen beacon-signals and a beacon was erected. It was to receive its warning from Beamsley Beacon and send it on to Scarcroft Moor (at Harewood) and Almscliff. A Beacon Keeper was resident on site from around 1799 in what became known as Jenny's Cottage. Recently the beacon has been lit at times of national celebration including coronations, jubilees and royal weddings. In later years Jenny's Cottage became a popular tea-room and source of evening entertainment.

Between 1967 and 1973 Messrs Arthur Gemmell, Reg Rawling, Eric Cowling and others including Edward Winpenny and N Whalley mounted a successful campaign to oppose the further quarrying of the Yorkgate site to break through the ridge. West Riding County Council had, in 1949, granted permission for a 250 metre wide gap to be cut through the escarpment extending 150 metres down the slope.

Management of the Chevin passed to Leeds City Council with Local Government re-organisation in 1974. Leeds began to extend the land holding of the park to secure more green space in what then became known as Chevin Forest Park. In 1977 Beacon Hill, the White House and White House Plantation were bought from the Sam Chippendale Foundation. An extensive programme of renovation ensued.

The Silver Jubilee celebrations of 1977 saw the beginning of a project, completed in 1978 by the Otley Rotary Club, to site a range-finder plaque at Beacon House. This gives bearings and distances to local landmarks in a 30-mile radius.

In 1979 Reg Rawling (pictured above) retired from his post to be succeeded by his son Keith.

Yorkgate Quarry became part of Chevin Forest Park in 1987 further securing its safety after the efforts of the campaign between 1967 and 1973. The status of the whole of Chevin Forest Park was safeguarded in 1989 when the park was designated a Local Nature Reserve in recognition of its particular value for the informal enjoyment of nature, its value for formal education and its high natural interest within the district.

The landholding of Chevin Forest Park was enhanced in 1995 with the purchase of Sinclair's Field.

A Forest Design Plan for the park was begun in July 1997 and providing a strategy for fifty years covering tree management, conservation, leisure activities and landscape design. The plan, in conjunction with the site's Management Plan, aims to improve Chevin Forest Park's conservation and amenity value and ensure good management for the future.

The management initiated by Reg Rawling has led to many awards being won over the years and these are listed in the timeline on the following pages.

Chevin Forest Park Timeline

972: The first written record of the Chevin when it was referred to as *'Scefinc'*. An article from the local press in 1960 reports Mr Frederick Morrell's speculation as to the origin of the name. He suggests that the word Chevin is derived from the pure British word *'cefn'*, a ridge or backbone. The modern Welsh name for a back (or ridge) is *'cefn'* (pronounced keven) and is very common in local names in Wales, this also applies to the Chevin of Otley, Chevin Hill near Derby, Chevington in Suffolk and Northumberland and also in Chevy Chase and the Cheviot Hills, each being a ridge or backbone of hills. Mr Morrell's conclusion was that the word Chevin was probably derived from the Cymric dialect of the Celtic language from which it is assumed that the name was first given/used 2,000 years ago.

1290: Danefield is mentioned as being part of the Forest of Knaresborough under the control of the King's Steward, John Fawkes.

1550: Caley Hall built as a residence for the Gascoignes of Gawthorpe near Harewood was occupied by Marmaduke, fourth son of Sir William Gascoigne, a grandson of Henry Percy, third Earl of Northumberland.

1611: George Gascoigne held Caley which was in the Manor of Pool. Died in 1626.

1628: Caley Hall was in the possession of John Dalton, a wealthy merchant from Hull. Died and buried in Otley Parish Church 1631.

1650: Caley Hall was owned by the Vavasour family.

1720: Henry Atkinson lived in Caley Hall. He married Frances Fawkes of Farnley Hall. Their son, Henry, died without issue 1751. The estate came to Fawkes.

1777: An extract from the Enclosure Act relating to Quarries by Commissioners appointed in the 18th year of the reign of King George the third:
'...and have ascertained and appointed and have hereby awarded the following parts of the said commons and waste lands, for and to be forever continued as stone quarries or places for the collecting of stone, that is to say one piece on parcel marked with the number 97 on the plan hereunto annexed, situated at a place called Pelstone Cross on Otley Chevin containing 3 acres 32 perches'

Early stone cutting was done by local men who lived in the Cambridge area of Otley. They are believed to have bought other large pieces of stone to the west of Pelstone from various allotment holders. They also laid a stone way across the bottom of Pelstone Crag which ended at a large quarry face on the border of Ritchies Plantation. An extraction road was laid down to East Chevin Road. It is believed this land was last worked for stone by locals circa 1920. The stone was used for the foundations of the Houses of Parliament, local houses and civic buildings, machine beds and roofing slates. The face of the quarry and a number of yards of quarry floor belong to Springfield Farm on East Chevin Road.

1791: Coaches began a service from Leeds to Settle via Otley and Headingley running once a week on

Friday. Fare was 21s 3d (£1.06). The route took coaches over the Chevin via East Chevin Road with passengers, on occasions, expected to walk up to the mounting block near Miller Lane.

1799: John Tillotson 'Beacon Keeper' tenant of 'Jenny's Cottage'.

1810-1825: The painter JMW Turner made many visits to Farnley Hall and the studies he made during these visits were a strong influence on his later works. At this time the Chevin was part of Farnley Hall Estate and stocked with deer, wild boar and even zebra.

c1830: Jenny Myers wife of John Myers, Shepherd for John Hartley, tenant of 'Jenny's Cottage'.

1856: '*We can hardly form a right idea of THE CHEVIN. It once abounded with precipitous rock work, and the general appearance was like the beautiful grandeur of Danfield (sic); it is often quoted in diaries, and journals, and excursions. You read in them of the ponderous crags of Chevin! of hardy travellers who had gained with thankfulness, its dizzy height! Now, most of the rocks are hid in tall plantations, or have been split, and used for buildings. So good is the stone of Chevin, that blocks were sent to London, having been tested by the best geologists, and now form the Foundations of the Houses of Parliament.*' Reverend J. Hart, 1856 Wharfedale Topography, antiquities and scenery.

1860: Jenny Miller tenant of "Jenny's Cottage". The road leading from East Chevin Road to Beacon Hill was named after her - 'Miller Lane'.

1865: White House Plantation and Ritchies Plantation planted. (According to RE Rawling. Ritchies Plantation was planted circa 1880.)

1883: Mr Veale from York, tenant of 'Jenny's Cottage'. He enlarged the cottage from two rooms and a dairy to refreshment rooms, and built 'Tea Pot Row', Leeds Road from the profits.

1939: Caley Hall bought by William Whiteley who lived there until 1958.

1939 - 1945: During the second world war many of the mature trees in Danefield and Caley Deer Park were felled to provide timber for the war effort. A contract dated 1 June 1942 indicates that 1,019 trees were sold to local timber merchants William Brear and Sons for £2,000.

1944: Otley Town Council accepted the gift of approx. 263 acres of land known as Danefield Wood and Deer Park from Major Le GGW Horton-Fawkes of Farnley Hall on Thursday 24th August at a special meeting of the Council.

1947: Mrs Laurence Jackson, daughter of John Blackburn, tenant of 'Jenny's Cottage'.

1952: Danefield Plantation and Poolscar planted.

1957: Poolscar partially replanted after fire.

1958: Reg Marston, tenant of 'Jenny's Cottage'.

1960s Keeper's Wood planted.

1960: Shawfield planted.

1960: 17th July Service of dedication for the memorial stone at Memorial Plantation. Caley Hall demolished.

1960/61: It is believed the White House was last inhabited.

1961: Deer Park planted and Foresters cabin built.

1964: Foxscar planted.

1965: Holbeck planted.

1966: Flint Wood planted.

1968: Quarry Wood planted. A lime tree donated by the Queen was planted at the head of Chippendale Ride as part of the 250th anniversary celebrations of the birth of Thomas Chippendale. Workshop added to foresters cabin. Lower Shawfield car park constructed.

1969 – 1971: Fred Atkinson leased the catering rights at 'Jenny's Cottage'.

1972: Sam Chippendale Foundation bought 'Jenny's Cottage' and Beacon Hill totalling 84 acres and the White House and Plantation totalling 13.4 acres.
1976: Middle Crag Wood planted. 'Jenny's Cottage' demolished and some of the stone used to build an extension to Hilton Grange Children's Home, Bramhope. The remaining stone was used to build Flower Fund homes at Guiseley.

1977: Cold Flatts planted. Leeds City Council bought the whole of Beacon Hill plus the White House Plantation from the Sam Chippendale Foundation. Beacon lit at Beacon Hill for Queen Elizabeth II's Silver Jubilee celebrations.

1979: Chevin Forest Park Ranger staff: Keith Rawling, Keith Groves and Miles Foulger. Manby Plantation acquired in June from Wharfedale Auction Mart.

1980: Cleaver Wood planted. 14 June White House Interpretative Centre opened at an official ceremony by Alwyn Ashley Town Mayor of Otley and Jose Alvarez Mayor of Montereau Fault-Yonne.

1981: 21 March: Keith Groves left. 30 March: Terry Cree started.

1982: September: Keith Rawling left to become Forestry Officer for L.C.C.

1983: January: Miles Foulger left to become Senior Ranger at Temple Newsam. March: Martin Parsons started.

1985: 1 October: Airey's Pig Farm acquired.

1986: In June: Martin Parsons left to become Senior Ranger at Middleton Park and Ian Watts started as Assistant Ranger. Chevin Watch Group started. Leader: Miss Barbara Winfield.

1987: 16 February: Springfield Wood acquired. 23 February first fencing work done in Yorkgate Quarry by CP Scheme and G Lomas. By 18 August Yorkgate Quarry had been acquired by Leeds. March: Richard Bowes first placement. Danefield won the Special Award Certificate in a Woodlands and Plantations competition run by the Royal Agricultural Society.

1988: July: Beacon lit in commemoration of 400th anniversary of defeat of the Spanish Armada.

1989: May: Ian Watts left. August: Richard Bowes started as Assistant Ranger. October: Chevin Forest Park designated a Local Nature Reserve. Chevin Volunteers group started. Awarded a Certificate of Merit in the

Duke of Cornwall's Award for Forestry and Conservation.

1994 Chevin declared a Centre of Excellence by the Forestry Authority. Award won in all categories; improving the quality of the landscape, providing access, creating benefits for wildlife and growing timber in environmentally friendly ways. Award presented by Ashley Jackson on 28 June.

1995: Sinclair's Field purchased from the Rose family with aid of donation from William Sinclair and Sons. August: Beacon lit in commemoration of the 50th anniversary of Victory in Japan day.

1996: February: White House Cafe closed after Mrs Poole failed to renew lease. September: Sinclair's Field opened together with orchard in memory of Jonathan Good.

1997: June: Won first prize in the class Judges Special Award of the Woodlands and Plantations Competition organised by the Royal Forestry Society of England, Wales and Northern Ireland on behalf of the Royal Agricultural Society of England. 4 June: Mr Reg Rawling, founder forester, died in Wharfedale General Hospital aged 88. December: Fencing works completed on the 'dog toiletting area' at Shawfield, provided to address the problems of dog fouling on the open field area of Shawfield.

1998: April 22: Unveiling of the geological interpretation panel at Beacon House explaining the geological features of the Wharfe valley and the Chevin. The panel was produced with assistance from the members of the Leeds Geological Association. The panel was unveiled by Professor Howel Francis, formerly assistant director of the British Geological Survey. May: Mr Paul Prince took on the tenancy of the White House Cafe. September: A Forest Design Plan for the park was completed after a period of work commencing in July 1997. The plan provides a strategy for the next 50 years covering tree management, conservation, leisure activities and landscape design. 7 September: Designation of Roman period native settlement in Danefield Wood as a Scheduled Ancient Monument. (Grid reference SE21874456 Monument number: SM31500). Designation of Roman period native settlement in Poolscar Wood as a Scheduled Ancient Monument. (Grid reference SE22174460. Monument number: 31501). December: Mr Paul Prince cancelled his tenancy of the White House Café.

1999: October. Foresters vacated cabins in Danefield and took up residence downstairs in the White House.

2000: Millennium beacon lit at Beacon House.February: Trees planted in Springfield meadow. As part of a scheme sponsored by Councillor Graham Kirkland in 1998/9 when he was Lord Mayor of Leeds, a tree was planted to represent each child of school age in Otley. The trees were planted by representative groups from all Otley schools except Prince Henry's. July: Flagged path across Beacon Hill completed.

2001: Chevin Forest Park closed for five weeks up to Easter as a result of foot and mouth disease.

Boats on the River Wharfe

The boats, which have been an integral part of the Otley scene for many years, were not seen in 2001 due to the Foot and Mouth restrictions. New Health and Safety Legislation has meant that discussions are taking place regarding the lease from Leeds City Council. It is hoped these will be resolved by the time of the Jubilee and Otley will see its boats back again.

Wharfemeadows, Otley.

Lentoid

Lentoid Plastics Ltd started trading in 1972 in Ashfield Works making glass lenses for spectacles. During the mid 70s, plastic lenses became available and they could fashion lighter and thinner lenses for a style conscious public. At the beginning of the 80s they moved to their Gay Lane factory that they still own. Computers and fax machines were in their infancy but they knew it was their only way forward in order to cut down on the many thousands of manual calculations that had to be made to turn an optician's prescription into something they could use on the shop floor. It was then that polycarbonate lenses came into production allowing police officers, paramedics and fire fighters to wear something virtually unbreakable in front of their eyes.

More recently, new techniques have given them better glass lenses but the bulk of their work is in plastic lenses. Their working methods have changed dramatically with the introduction of computers, leaving more time to devote to the cosmetic side of spectacle lenses. However, the theory behind lenses is still centuries old and some machinery is decades old because newer equipment with its modern electronics cannot do the job. One of their companies has invented a special fitting to surfacing machines which is patented and known in the USA and Australia as 'The Otley'.

They have made lenses for all sorts of uses including automatic train protection systems, EuroDisney telescopes and decorative tables. Specialising in difficult work they supply the whole of the British Isles and parts of Europe with ophthalmic lenses as well as scientific and technical lenses.

For the last few years their retail shop at their Gay Lane factory has been open to the public. They manufacture all types of lenses from single vision to bifocal to varifocal, from white glass to colours and tints and in photochromic materials. If it's technically possible, they've probably made it!

Organisations

Otley Brass Band

Otley has had more than one brass band over the years but the current band was set up by Norman Boothroyd in 1974. His daughter still plays with them, along with 27 other instrumentalists of varying abilities and ages. Rehearsals are held, and new music is learnt for Spring and Autumn concerts and for entertainment in surrounding parks over the summer months. They join forces with the Buttercross Belles and Otley Choral Society outside the Woolpack at Christmastide.

Edgar Kennedy, an extremely accomplished musician, is the musical director in 2002. Over recent years, the band has gone from strength to strength and though they do not compete, they are a good section three band. They were nominated as an Otley Carnival Beneficiary in 2000. They used this fund to purchase new instruments, donating those replaced to local schools.

Otley Folk Club

The Otley Folk Club was started at the New Inn by Phil Frazer and Martin Carter during the late 60's. Around 1980, the Leather Bottle Club was held at the New Inn. Ian Glover, Tony McGrath and 'Trog' were the organisers, encouraging local singers and booking excellent, and sometimes, unusual national and international artists.

From about 1985, Otley Folk Club was established at the Yeoman by Rick Peacock. Subsequent moves were back to the New Inn until its closure, to The Whitakers Arms, The Three Horse Shoes and then to The Black Horse where Rick stood down in 1998. The Club subsequently moved back to the Three Horse Shoes to be run by Steve Fairholme and supported by Malcolm Devereux. The high quality of local regular performers, along with a variety of booked guests, ensures good entertainment. The 'famous' Last Orders folk band sprang from the folk club in about 1990: still going strong in 2002.

The Otley Folk Festival, started in 1991, is a direct product of the Folk Club.

Otley Little Theatre Club

Otley Little Theatre Club was formed in 1939 and has been providing local entertainment ever since. In the early days it concentrated on 'straight' plays; we still perform two plays each season, but in recent years our pantomimes and musical shows have also become popular events in Otley's calendar. Our productions in 2001-2002 are 'Comfort and Joy' by Mike Harding, 'Cinderella' by Norman Robbins, 'The Hollow' by Agatha Christie and 'Prohibition', a musical show based on 1930s America.

There are 55 members and 68 patrons. Our centre of activity is Otley Civic Centre, where we rehearse two or three times a week, often finishing up in 'The Manor' pub nearby. We have a diary of popular social events such as play-readings, a treasure hunt, the annual dinner, an Oscars evening and quizzes (this year's took the form of 'The Weakest Link'). Each year we participate in the Wharfedale Festival of Theatre.

Ramblers Association

The group was formed some 30 years ago primarily as a 'working footpath group' to improve the state of the footpaths in the Washburn and Lower Wharfedale area. It also organises family rambles to familiarise people with the extensive local footpath network.

Projects that helped this policy along include the original Ilkley Moor Footpath Map, done as a joint project with Bradford Ramblers, and the original Washburn Valley Footpath Map for the Ramblers Association West Riding Area Publicity Committee. The latter was innovative in that it was printed on hardwearing waterproof plastic.

Significant campaigns have been:

The provision of the Chevin Link Footbridge across the Otley bypass. Protests at the original plan to run the M1/A1 link from Pudsey to Dishforth (which would have destroyed swathes of green belt around Horsforth, Rawdon, Bramhope and the Lower Wharfe Valley). Owler Park (Ilkley) diversion path through the beautiful Bluebell Wood. Other successful actions against proposals for development in Green Belt areas such as the proposal to erect a large building near a footpath in high Green Belt land in the Wharfe Valley. For this, a protest walk was held and a video sequence was presented to the planning committee to illustrate the intrusion of the building on the surrounding countryside.

The group strongly supports the present campaign for building a footbridge across the River Wharfe at Burley in Wharfedale – planning permission for which has already been obtained. This would provide a safe year round crossing point at the existing right of way, which at present goes over the worn and dangerous stepping stones. The splendid footpath networks on both sides of the river would be then safely linked and some short, family walks would be possible from Otley to Ilkley, using public transport facilities to return.

Every day problems of blocked paths and broken stiles have to be dealt with all the time – and these very rarely make the news.

Manor Social Club

What is probably one of Otley's oldest social clubs recently celebrated its 100th birthday having been formed on 28 January 1902 as a Business and Gentlemen's club, on the top floor of the Old Grammar School in Manor Square, Otley (now a Grade 2 listed building). In its prominent position looking up Kirkgate it soon attracted many of the familiar names of the businesses in Otley at that time. It provided a quiet meeting room, with bar facilities, card tables etc and a snooker table, the receipt for which is still proudly displayed in the club. During the second world war, it was used by army officers who were stationed at Farnley camp and treated as 'guests'.

More recently, the facilities have been used by the Otley Rotary club for 'Games Evenings' against other clubs, and for meetings by the Royal Air Force Association, the Chamber of Trade and Commerce and for three years was a popular and appropriate venue for the 'Music Hall' acts during the Otley Black Sheep Folk Festival. Ladies, however, were only admitted on Friday afternoons for tea. The club's presidents have included Mr. Frank Lofthouse and Mr. Fred Whyte but the list will now be coming to its end as the club will be closing down in July 2002, with Mr. Edward Winpenny as its last president. The building which for many years was the home of 'Manor China', has now been sold and permission given for it to be changed into offices.

Weston Lane Junior Sports and Social Club

The pavilion was constructed as a community clubhouse in 1959 by fund raising on the estate and help from local businesses.

Due to the hard work of Len Wetherill, Dick Hay and Harry Dorling, the club ran a range of social and sporting programmes in the 60s. This was carried on by Eric Shaw from the 60s to mid 90s with soccer being very successful.

In 2001 disaster struck when an arsonist set fire to the green wooden building.

The fledgling club and its new Pavilion in 1958.

The club is now re-grouping and re-building with Chris Laison as Chairman. This has been made possible by insurance money with help from the Lions, Freemasons, a CIT grant and other individuals including a fund-raising group led by Maureen Thackwray.

Otley Social Working Men's Club

This club was started in 1959. The founder members of Dick Hay, George Reddyhoff and Joe Wilkins, first considered the idea in the yard of the Urban District Council where they worked. A committee was formed in George's pre-fab on Weston Ridge. The UDC. was approached for the land and Vaux Breweries provided a loan to finance the building. Some of the members also helping to raise funds for the junior sports club.

The loan was repaid over the years but the club has maintained a reputation for fund-raising. In 1988 Gerry Braithwaite (current President) began a fund emanating from the loss of his daughter's baby due to heart disease. Over the years some £40,000 has been raised by members, both within the club and from various sponsored events.

The club is forward looking and in 1997 established equality for women. Mrs Mandy Cater, as secretary, has spent a great deal of time and effort in obtaining sponsorship for their charities. Membership is currently more than 600.

Buttercross Belles and Wayzgoose Morris Teams

Annual events include Mother's Day at a local venue such as Harewood House or Fountain's Abbey. May Day involves dancing up the dawn on Otley Chevin on 1 May followed by children's maypole dancing in Otley late afternoon. Boxing Day is the team's firm favourite with friends and families at The Woolpack. The Belles also support Otley events such as the Carnival, Folk Festival and Victorian Fayre.

The Buttercross Belles is a women's Morris team or side who dance mainly in a lively NorthWest style. Team members wear tap shoes as opposed to clogs with a distinctive kit comprising a white short-sleeved dress over which is a green smock trimmed with purple. A decorated straw hat or 'Alice band' completes the picture.

Jenny Liston and a group of enthusiastic friends founded the team in January 1992. Jenny had been a member of Betty Lupton's Ladle Lakers, a women's Morris side from Harrogate and wished to form a similar group in Otley. The Belles made their debut at Westgate School on 1 May 1992 with only two dances to their name but have gone from strength to strength during the succeeding ten years.

The Buttercross Belles practise each Thursday evening between 8pm and 10pm at St Joseph's School, Manor Square, Otley. Some of the team's children practise during the year for special occasions such as May Day Maypole Dancing and Boxing Day. New dancers and musicians are welcome to join the Belles each September.

In addition to the annual events the team dances throughout the year at a variety of local and national events. Previous years have seen the Belles venture across the Channel to Normandy while in July 2002 the team is off to Switzerland. The Belles (pictured below with Paddy Steval in Montereau) are currently involved in the Otley Maypole Restoration Project.

Otley is rich in Morris sides for as well as the Belles there are three other teams: Wharfedale Wayzgoose are a mixed Border Morris side who wear multi-coloured tatter jackets and paint their faces black and white; Kitchen Taps are a lively women's Appalachian side with bright costumes and tap shoes; Flash Company dress in yellow and black and include several styles of Morris in their dancing

Community Play Association

Otley Community Play Association is a registered charity which was formed in 1994 to put on a large-scale community play. The preparation over two years included fund-raising, publicity, workshops in writing, acting and music, research and rehearsals. Over three hundred people took part in 'The Heart Shaped Field', which was performed on eleven nights in April 1996 and was an outstanding success. The enthusiasm generated by the play carried over into the creation of a community choir (Otley Singers), a drama group (Otley Community Players, which now has a group for young people, OY! theatre) and a group dedicated to the establishment of an Arts Centre in the town (Arts for Otley - now The Courthouse Project).

Otley Ladies Lifeboat Guild

It may be just about as far from the sea as you can get in Yorkshire but Otley Ladies Lifeboat Guild has an impressive record of raising funds for the RNLI, which relies on voluntary efforts to carry out its hugely worthwhile work. The actual history of the Guild is uncertain. It is known that Lady Duncan, of Otley, was an active member of the Bradford Guild and was presented in 1936 with a statuette in silver of a lifeboatman. This is now used as the chairman's badge of office. The Otley Guild closed down and its minute books were lost but it was reformed under the auspices of Mrs William Sinclair and Mrs Harry Sharp, who is still a member. Today the Guild is flourishing with a small hardworking committee which raises thousands of pounds each year. Successful events have included a hot fish pie supper with Peter Race, coxswain of the Teesmouth lifeboat, as speaker. Every year a fashion show and bridge drive are held along with coffee mornings and a bigger event is usually run near Christmas. In 2001 the Harrogate Male Voice Choir attracted a full house at Pool village hall. The present president is Anne Lister, with Rita Swallow as chairman, Angela Mason secretary and Wendy Holt treasurer. Mrs Doreen Turner, who stepped down two years ago as president after holding most offices on the committee, has been awarded the RNLI's silver badge in recognition of her service. Margaret Newby, who is still on the committee, was similarly recognised after raising thousands of pounds as souvenir sales secretary.

Handbell & Chime Orchestra

This group was founded by Mike and Carole Charnley in 1989, and is an active member of the Handbell Ringers of Great Britain organisation. The aim of their group is to bring the uniquely British art of handbell tune ringing, in all its forms, to the public.

For many years handbells have been locked away in church towers, only seeing the light of day at Christmas or other special times of the church year. Today's groups have larger sets of bells and comprehensive repertoires.

They won a 5–octave set of Malmark handbells and a 2-octave set of Schulmerich hand chimes, with which they perform as soloist, duettists and ensembles. Their group has performed in many places and for many events, including performing at Harewood House.

The Group has even gone international – taking part in the Sixth International Hand bell Ringers Symposium in Adelaide, Australia, in 1994.
They also have Junior teams at St Joseph's RC and Farnley C of E Schools, and their own Otley Junior Bell and Chime Orchestra – who have won many awards at Harrogate Music Festival. St Joseph's have also won the WMF Millennium Cup at Ilkley.

Otley Chamber of Trade & Commerce

Founded in the 1930s to promote, improve and secure trading interests for Otley and district, it provides a forum for the exchange of current information relating to business in the town. The Chamber was the original promoter of the Victorian Fayre and Chevin Fell Race. It is a member of the Town Partnership.

Otley and District Retired Men's & Women's Forums

Started in 1962. Two separate retired peoples' forums meeting fortnightly on a social basis to receive speakers covering a wide range of cultural topics. Their motto being 'Fraternity and Enlightenment'.

Services

Police

The origins of our police system may be found in tribal laws and customs of the Saxon invaders. The *'tything'* system was a personal and local one in which all members of the community accepted an obligation for the discipline of each other. Freemen unless specifically excused were enrolled for police purposes into groups of ten families known as *tythings*, each headed by a *tythingman*. If any member of the tything committed a crime the others had to produce him for trial. Should they fail, then they as a group could be called on to make compensation. It was the *tythingman's* duty to raise a posse to pursue the offender and bring him for trial. Groups of *tythings* were formed into hundreds with a royal reeve as headman, who exercised administrative and judicial powers through a hundred court. The term of duty in Otley was for three years and it appears to have been an onerous one, as in 1306 the archbishop was compelled to distrain upon the goods of a reeve who had died in office, to the amount of £10 approximately, a large sum of money in those days.

The timeline on the following page highlights development from 1361 to date:

1361: The Knights of the Shires became Justices of the Peace, which was to continue for several centuries.

1400-1600: Parish constables appear, controlled by the vestry. Important unit of local administration in Tudor times.

1750: Henry Fielding at Bow Street formed a body of six men, later to become known as Bow Street Runners.

1785: Pitt the Younger's Bill provided for the establishment of a strong police force to act throughout the whole of metropolitan London.

1800: Formation of Thames River police due to so much crime amongst the docks area.

1805: Bow Street patrol extended nation-wide.

1829: The Metropolitan Police Act. New Scotland Yard commenced. Peel's new police 'Peelers' or 'Bobbies'.

1856: County and Borough Police Act. Its limit of one constable per 1,000 population relaxed so that a greater ratio of police could be obtained. This act led to formation of the West Yorkshire Constabulary.

1856: Chief Constable's report for the period states: 'on the night of 20 March a Constable Walker was attacked and stabbed in eight places whilst attempting to apprehend some sheep stealers'.

1874: Court House and Police Station built, Courthouse Street, Otley.

1893: Mounted branch. Typical duty appears to be reporting traffic offences (usually dray-men asleep in charge of their horses).

1906: Fingerprinting begins.

1928: Wireless introduced.

1930: First patrol car; Jowett 7h.p. Touring cars. Nicknamed 'Blood Tubs'. With the passing of the Road Traffic Act, traffic law was regularised.

1934: Detective training.

1938: Road traffic division.

1944: Driving school.

1946: Police women.

1951: Police dog patrols.

1960: Motor cycle patrols for country beats.

1964: Vans replace motor cycles. Present police station built in the grounds of the Manor House. Traffic wardens appear in Otley. Personal radios introduced, which has probably had largest influence of all changes. Amalgamation of seven forces. Otley made administrative headquarters for the Otley division, which extends from North Yorkshire boundary down to Leeds inner ring road. The area is some 35,000 acres with a population of some 300.000 served by a police force of 300 constables – approximately a similar ratio to that of 1856.

1977: PC Dave Robson, Otley community Police Officer for many years received The Chief Constable's commendation.

1985: PC Dave was instrumental in the setting up of the first neighbourhood watch scheme in the county 2001 102 schemes covering 1567 members are running in Otley.

Police archive records end in 1985. The police dog section which used Alsatians have added other breeds that are better suited for drug and explosive searches. There have been changes in uniform, issue of new truncheons and body vests. There is a full time underwater search and rescue team. Task Force Teams, armed response vehicles, drugs teams, force helicopter, and graded response service have all been implemented in the last 25 years. Video surveillance is helping to catch criminals and there is a call to cover more of the town centre, not just the bus station.

1993: Mick McManus became the World Bathtub Paddling Champion. A disease-free elm tree has been planted in the grounds of the police station. The courthouse has been closed and all cases transferred to Leeds. The police station is virtually closed with control transferred to Weetwood.

1996: Courthouse closed after 122 years. Cases now dealt with in Leeds

Telephone

The first telephone communication service to Otley was by the National Telephone Company in 1896. This was an amalgamation of private companies. Mounsey stationers at 13 Kirkgate housed the exchange.

In the early 80s mobile phones became a reality for the general public. They were the size and weight of a brick with a long retractable aerial and very expensive. Good reception was only available in the London area. Now they are the size of a small bar of chocolate with integral aerial. They cost between £80 and £200. As well as speaking to friends world wide, you can text message them, send e-mails, play computer games, access the Top 10, and access information via WAP. For a long time Otley was a black spot for reception due to the Chevin. Since a mast was erected at the cattle market on Leeds Road two companies have good reception and the others have better reception as new masts are erected in the area but reception is patchy in some areas of the town.

1901: Exchange moved to Old Vicarage Church Lane.

1912: The Post Office took over private companies.

1923: The GPO acquired a May Note telephone exchange.

1942: The exchange moved to the upstairs of the new Post Office building.

1946: Equipment changed to automatic exchange.

1964: STD introduced to Otley.

1965: Otley telephone exchange responsibility and routing transferred to Bradford from Leeds.

1973: International direct dialling which gave Otley subscribers direct access to 80% of the world's telephones.

1977: Otley had 3,850 lines and approximately 5,700 telephones (including extensions)

1979: Opening of a Crossbar exchange in Charles Street with a capacity of 7,000 lines. Introduction of six digit numbers starting 46.

1981: British Telecom set up as a separate corporation from the Post Office.

Until 1985, Kineholm, the former residence of the Duncan family, was the North East regional training school for telephone engineers. The house was acquired by the GPO in 1938. It is said that Lloyd George slept there; the windows in the entrance hall depicted Aesop's Fables in stained glass, and the garden was supposed to have held one of every type of tree growing in Europe. The training school was moved to Harrogate in 1985, the land was sold, the buildings demolished, and the area redeveloped with housing.

Otley's Postal Services

Otley's postal services are closely linked to Leeds. In 1977 the mail posted in Otley was sorted at the mechanised sorting office in Royal Mail House, Wellington Street, Leeds, In 2002 mail from Otley is collected and sorted by the staff of the new sorting office at Yeadon. Mail for delivery in Otley is sorted at Nelson Street.

Otley's earliest importance as a postal centre was due to the fact that it was the junction town on the mail routes from Leeds to Lancashire via Skipton and from Newcastle to the South via Wetherby. Records in 1822 state that the East-West coach arrived at 5.00pm and departed at 2.30am, while the North South coach arrived at 2.30am and departed at 5.00pm. Thus an interchange of mailbags was possible. All mail carriers were then contractors of the government.

Earliest information on the postal service in Otley can be gained from the Parish records. In April 1797 a meeting of inhabitants considered 'the most eligible mode of conveyance of a daily post from Leeds to Otley'. William Garnett and William Marchbank were to solve the problem with the Postmaster for Leeds.

Six years later, at a similar parish meeting, arrangements were made for a twice-daily post, on horseback to Wetherby, at 7.00am and 4.00pm. Mr George Blackburn, the Otley Post Master, having made arrangement with the Wetherby Post Master. Every letter was charged at 1d extra to the postal charge. It is interesting to note that the postmaster was appointed by the inhabitants of Otley and could not be removed as long as

he gave satisfaction to the said inhabitants. This practice continued until 1937 when Otley became a sub-post office of Leeds. At the time of the Queen's accession postage was 2 1/2d (1p). Costs have risen: in 1976 we paid 6p or 8p with a choice of first or second class mail, 2002 we pay 19p or 27p. In 1828 the accepted delivery charges from Otley to Skipton were 5d (2p)and from Wetherby to Otley 4d. The early 1840s saw letters franked 'Otley Penny Post' and two hand stamps were assigned to Otley.

There have been many changes in the services provided to the general public in the last 50 years. Many bewail the increased costs and the reduction in the number of collections and deliveries. The postal coding has been put to effective use.

The major change since 1952 has been the change of status of the Post Office, which became a public corporation in 1969. We have also seen the introduction of several specialised services:

Datapost for the business community, and Giro, the Post Office Banking Service. In 1964 it was decided to issue more special sets of stamps for important anniversaries, events of national and international importance and to reflect Britain's contribution to world affairs.

1981: The telecommunications services became a new corporation British Telecom.

1987: The Post Office's counters business of high street post offices became a limited company.

1990: Parcelforce was launched as an independent division with full control of its operations.

Girobank was sold to Alliance and Leicester Building Society.

1999: January The Post Office acquired its first foreign acquisition with the take-over of German Parcel, to date 16 other acquisitions have been made.

2001: The Post Office becomes plc: the Post Office Group name changes to Consignia, but the business brand names stay the same – Royal Mail, Parcelforce Worldwide and Post Office for the network of high street post offices.

The Post Office building site has been moved several times from the Market place to Manor Square, to 54 Boroughgate and finally in 1942 to Nelson Street. Several sub-post offices were opened during the early 1900s. In 2002 there are two sub-Post Offices Westbourne on Bradford Road and Newall on Weston Lane.

Fire Service

The early beginnings are not very clear. However, on the death of a certain David Chippendale in 1860, valuation shows he was in possession of a manual fire engine, piping, buckets and hats.

Upon the forming of the Local Board in 1864, it appears that they acquired these items.

1866: A crew of twelve is listed with duties, none of which had a trade connected with mechanics.

1875: Mrs Emma Dawson presented another manual engine (in her letter she declines a steam engine, as it was pointed out that an engineer would be required to operate it). She included uniforms and axes for the men.

1894: There is reference to the Local Board borrowing money to buy a fire engine. It would appear very likely that this was the Shand Mason Steamer illustrated in the Otley Museum.

1884: The Firestation logbook shows a report of only two fires being attended.

1887: Five calls received.

1914: Marks a major advancement with the introduction of a motorised fire engine.

1915: Saw a Zeppelin raid in the area with a few bombs dropped at Harewood with no damage. A Mr Ivan King, who went to watch the fireman fighting a rabbit hutch blaze on the Pool Road in 1927 was voluntarily roped into help and subsequently, became a driver. His annual retention fee was twenty-five shillings (£1.25) plus one shilling and nine pence per hour (9p), attendance allowance. He then stayed on as a part-time fireman until he retired in 1960 as fire chief.

1930: Saw the most spectacular fire when the candle works in Station Road was set alight. It was a major hazard in those days as the principal means of extinguishing a fire was with the use of water. Foam was a new idea and in limited supply. The fire was very difficult to put out with molten transparent wax pouring down Station Road and around

the corner into Bondgate. Many people are reported as being burnt by stepping upon it in mistake for water. The most serious aspect of this flowing wax was that it entered the drainage system whence it solidified. This necessitated considerable work in digging up Kirkgate and re-laying the drains.

1937: Fire at Patricks Wood Yard of creosoted timber, a very big blaze.

1938: At about this time new appliances were provided.

1950: Large fire in Danefield Wood which took 44 hours to put out.

1954: Second candle works fire less serious this time due to foam equipment.

1956: A busy year with a large mill fire at Keighley, 8 people killed.

Fire station moved to Bondgate from Courthouse Street. Now part of the West Riding fire service. New fire engines were provided. Another 13-hour fire on the Danefield estate.

1962: Bramhope fire: sixty-six pigs died.

1967: Mossdale Cavern pothole disaster, helped with pumping.

1973: Pocket alerts replace siren call out.

1975: Dibbles Bridge bus crash: 32 dead.

1976: 213 fire calls compared with 2 in 1884.

1979: A fire at William Sinclair's caused damage estimated at £250,000

1982: 40 firemen tackled a blaze at Duncan Craft workshops. Former Tannery of Wm Barker & Sons was destroyed by fire during the night. A fire at Smith Settle in Otley Mills, the business was unaffected.

1989: Former Tannery of William Barker & Sons was destroyed by fire during the night. A fire at Smith Settle in Otley Mills: the business was unaffected.

1990: 75 year old Florrie Nutter died in her sheltered bungalow following a fire.

1991: A fire broke out in the laundry at Prince Henry Grammar School.

1992: Stock worth up to £35,000 was damaged by a fire at Olley of Otley.

1992 : Otley Fire station made a one engine unit. Fire at the Storerooms in Otley Mills rented by John Stewart. Former Headmaster's house at Prince Henry's School was set on fire causing £35,000 damage.

1993: Minister of the United Reform Church Bridge Street watched the church hall burn down on the 25th Anniversary of his induction. A fire at R.G.Fowlers, timber merchants, in Albion Street was caused by internal combustion in a machine. Fire badly damaged Esquire hairdressing salon in Bridge Street. Chippendale School fire - books and equip-

Opposite: Station Officer and Crew with old Dennis appliances - 1987

ment were destroyed. A fire at Otley's former open-air swimming pool was attended by Otley and Rawdon fire fighters. Dog escaped from fire at Otley Private Hire Taxi office.

1996: A blaze gutted the Falcon Club in Beech Hill in the early hours of the morning. A 3 litre Jaguar belonging to Dr Waters burst into flames at the Wesley Street lights.

1997: Otley fire fighters were on the lookout for two more persons to join their team.

1999: A fire broke out at Dress Circle in Station Road. A chimney at Chevin Fish Shop, Boroughgate, caught fire.

2000: An allotment blaze behind Garnetts Mill sparked fury among plot-holders. Fire fighters battled a blaze at Otley Paper Mill. A fire in a toilet at Prince Henry's Grammar School caused damage estimated at £1,000. Weston Lane Junior Sports & Social club was gutted by fire.

2001: A fire broke out at Strands, hairdressers, Manchester Square. Otley Fire fighters raised funds to help the,New York Fire-fighters and Families Appeal, following 11 September 2001 New York disaster.

Ambulance

When Her Majesty Queen Elizabeth II celebrated her Silver Jubilee in 1977, the county's ambulance service was centred around its new headquarters at Threelands, Birkenshaw which were officially opened on 8th September 1971.

At that time the county was served by 24 ambulance stations, six agency services and the hospital car service which together conveyed an average of 739,400 patients and covered 4,945,343 miles per annum.

From its headquarters in Bradford, West Yorkshire Metropolitan Ambulance Service serves a diverse geographical area from the very rural Yorkshire Dales to the urban conurbations of Leeds and Bradford: around 2.1 million people.

The nearest ambulance station to Otley is Bradford Road, Menston. WYMAS is operationally responsible for the Yorkshire Air Ambulance, which is a charity-funded service based at Leeds Bradford Airport.

The dedication of WYMAS has been recognised by the recent granting of Charter Mark status for both the Ambulance Services and Telecare Directorate which includes NHS Direct and NHS Professionals as a developing service. It is the second time this prestigious honour which recognises good practice in public services has been awarded to WYMAS.

Records

Since 1977, the centralisation of the archive records of our public services have fallen by the wayside. Some were even destroyed. This has made it particularly difficult to get information on telephones and the police in the past quarter century.

Gas

In 1836 a Society was established in Otley to contribute in certain proportions towards the purchase of ground and the erection of buildings and apparatus for the purpose of making gas and therewith lighting mills, houses and other places in the township. The Society was called. The Otley Gas and Coke Company and there were 400 shares of £5.

Thirty years later the coke was dropped and the Otley Gas Company was formed.

Quite naturally the people from nearby villages wanted light too, and in 1889 the Otley Gas Company was empowered to supply gas to Newall-with-Clifton, Farnley and Weston.

1901 OTLEY GAS ACT. The Act stated that due to the increasing demand for gas in the district supplied by the Company it was expedient that the Company s works and mains should be extended and improved. To achieve that the Company was dissolved. Then its members were united into a new company that went under the same name. The Otley Gas Company. Everything of the old company was vested in the new Company. The limits of supply remained the same. In fact the Company continued without alteration, from that rather pointless day in 1901 until nationalisation in May 1949.

Early 1970 saw Gas engineers converting every gas appliance and meter in the Otley area ready for the introduction of North Sea Gas later in the year.

Since privatisation in 1986 The State owned British Gas has been deregulated and divided into three main companies. Lattice which includes, Transco Provides energy services-Leasing-property operations and telecom. Centrica, a consumer facing business selling gas, and other services under the British Gas brand. British Gas is a company involved in exploration and provision of gas.

Transco being responsible for gas pipeline network has been visible in Otley replacing many old steel pipes with modern yellow plastic pipes. During 2001 in the Leeds area 24,000 meters of mains were replaced at the cost of £2:6million.

Otley's gasholder was decommissioned in 2000 having been in use since 1900. It diameter was 85ft with walls 20ft high. It has been demolished and the land decontaminated.

Otley under flood water in 2002

Water

Otley received its first piped water supply in 1761 when Nathaniel Aked, Enoch Neal and William Maude combined to construct a system. The water originally came from a spring on the Goosehands Park of the Chevin, and was added to later by diverting Dennwell beck, then feeding back to the reservoir below the old Leeds Road. This was then extended via a storage tank at the bottom of the hill and wooden pipes, to the Bondgate – Boroughgate and Kirkgate areas of Otley. The water being dispersed by cistern and hand pumps. Westgate was supplied from Stokswell, at the Western part of the Chevin, together with a piped supply from Springfields place at the foot of Bradford Road. Hence the Piper Lane from the days of wooden pipes.

Because of the increase in population, the need for bigger and better supplies was being felt by the middle of the 19th Century. In 1885 the Board was granted powers under the Otley Local Board Act to construct further works to impound water from Gooseland Well in Menston and to convey it to the town via a new main running along Bradford Road to Westgate. But as the population continued to grow, the Otley Urban District Council, which had superseded the local Board in 1894, wisely felt they ought to secure an even better supply for the new century. They obtained powers in an Act of 1900 to construct March Ghyll Reservoir at Middleton, to the north of Ilkley.

This reservoir, which had a capacity of 87 million gallons was completed in 1906. It was Otley's principal source of supply until 1996. The water was treated at source by pressure filters and supplies were given to the various villages on the route between Middleton and Otley. In 1962 the responsibility for the Otley supplies passed to Rombalds Water Board, and in1973 along with 200 other Council bodies was brought together to form The Yorkshire Water Authority. This was privatised in the 1990's to become Yorkshire Water PLC. Supplying Yorkshire with more than 1240 million litres a day and disposing of 1:7 cubic meters of sewage each day. The source of Yorkshire's water is half stored in reservoirs a third is taken from rivers and the rest pumped from natural underground sources.

To meet higher standards of water quality Otley is now supplied with water from the new (1993) Graincliffe treatment plant above Bingley. This is a multi-stage water treatment plant, taking its source water, either from the River Wharfe and upland reservoirs, or from Eccup reservoir. Eccup is supplied from the Washburn valley reservoirs and from the river Ouse above York. Being able to change the source of supply to Graincliffe gives added security during periods of drought. A £350 million grid transfers the water across Yorkshire. Yorkshire Water PLC is continually working on upgrading Victorian cast iron pipes and others by removing corrosion and relining the pipes consequently improving water quality, and decreasing water loss.

Sewage from Otley goes to the sewage treatment plant on the banks of the Wharfe, between Otley and Pool, before disposal of the effluent into the river.

Yorkshire Water publishes walk packs (2002 price £2:00) covering the North Peaks, South

Pennines and Nidderdale. They contain long and short walks around various reservoirs. Yorkshire Water donated a computer to Otley All Saints Infant School 2001. They also support Yorkshire Otters and river project and the Red Kite restoration project.

Electricity

Electricity first came to Otley in 1920. In those days the supply was in the hands of private supply companies and municipal authorities, the nearest of these being the Leeds and Bradford electricity supply departments.

Otley surprisingly took its supply from the Yorkshire Electric Power Company who at that time operated from Ferrybridge (A) at Thornhill. Their 11,000-volt A.C. supply terminated in Rodley. Underground cables then brought the supply to a sub-station in Beech Hill, where it was transformed down to the domestic 230v.

The demand must have been small having an upper limit of 400kw (400x1 Bar electric fires). 1976 demand is 14,000kw, an increase of 3,500% in the 56 years since 1921. The original four sub-stations have been modified and increased to 41, although part of the old underground cable that came via Rawdon is still in use.

In 1937 the output from Thornhill was increased to 33,000 volts and a new sub-station established at Chevin End. This was subsequently uprated to receive 66,000 volts from Ferrybridge (A). The steel mast overhead line that provided that supply still stands along the top of the Chevin.

The new route for the Yorkshire Electricity Board bulk supply is via Menston. This supply is tied into the national grid by means of a 132,000-volt overhead line connexion from Bradford since 1966. The supply enters Otley at 33000 volts at the North Avenue sub-station.

For those of you who are wondering how the early trolley buses fitted into the Otley electricity supply system, the answer is they did not. The trolley bus service operated from Whitecross, Guiseley, and was powered by a D.C. supply from Leeds Corporation.

Following the privatisation of the Electricity Industry in England and Wales, Yorkshire Electricity began trading on 31/3/1990 taking over YEB's activities. There have been no major changes to Otley's supply in the last 25 years.

Passenger Transport

The public passenger service, apart from the railway system of the mid nineteenth century, began when Leeds City Tramways inaugurated a trackless tram service between Otley and Guiseley, the first tram to Otley being on Monday 30th August 1915, using the May Pole as the turn-round. The service was withdrawn in 1928, and the last tram left on 28th August.

The firm of Barrett and Thornton began a bus service in 1920, starting from the bottom of Burras Lane to Lawnswood, connecting with Leeds trams. The vehicles were 10 and 20 seater Fords, entered from the rear, with a seat on each side, the passengers facing each other. The service was half hourly and the fare 6d (2p).

Later, William Skinner entered into competition on the Leeds route, using a Ford charabanc complete with hood. The stand was Manor Square to the Black Swan, Leeds, the fare 8d (3p). This firm dropped out when Coles and Yates extended the service to Ilkley, with a 'picking up stop' at the Bowling Green, Otley.

Barrett and Thorntons eventually came into the hands of Samuel Ledgard of Armley, who later took over Tate's cream buses to Ilkley. The West Yorkshire Car Co. bought the service of Coles and their Leeds, Otley and Ilkley route in 1928.

The first service to Harrogate was begun by N Robinson of Otley about 1921-22, his stand being in front of the Conservative Club. This was later operated by Blyth and Berwick, using Chevrolets, who extended the service from Harrogate to Bradford. In 1928 this firm was taken over by Ledgards. In this period, Harrogate Road Car Co. were also running 'Tilling Stevens' between Otley and Harrogate.

In 1921 Frank Blakey, a local carrier, started a service to Shipley (later to Bradford) from Manor Square, and Mrs Buttery of Otley began a service to Ilkley about 1923. Eventually each service was absorbed one with another, until only Ledgards and the West Yorkshire Co. remained, and these two companies combined to build Otley Bus Station in 1938.

In the early 80s the Passenger Transport Act de-regulated trains and buses. Once again for a short period we saw multiple operators on routes. The bus station was reduced in size in the late 80's as the Orchardgate development took shape.

In the mid 90s Government legislation permitted town councils to subsidise public transport for the first time. In 1999 following a long period of negotiation the Town Council signed an agreement with the Passenger Transport Authority, which saw the introduction of a whole series of measures including the introduction of a popular 'Hoppa' service linking the town with Menston railway station.

Cross party support on Otley Town Council has also seen proposals for the return of the railway to Otley – for the first time since the Beeching cuts of the 1960's. In 2001 the Passenger Transport Authority announced that feasibility work was underway.

Otley's 'Market Towns Initiative' status, announced in 2001, is also due to see a big boost to local bus services, including the introduction of a 'yellow bus' scheme for local school children, and improved services to the town's hospital.

Otley - The charity Capital of the North

Otley boasts eleven charity shops staffed by many volunteers. It is a reflection of the town's economic fortunes that so many shops are empty and available for charities to occupy.

After a hard day of **CANCER RESEARCH** I had a **MIND** to walk in **OTLEY** with **SUE RYDER**. Walking would give us plenty of **SCOPE** to give our **HEARTS** a good **FOUNDATION** and would definitely **HELP THE AGED**! If we got into any trouble we could always count on the **RED CROSS**. Unfortunately, whilst on our walk, our dog which came from the **RSPCA** became lame. Ironic that we should just be outside the **PDSA**! After our tiring walk we called in at **ST GEMMAS** for a rest whilst we waited for our "**OXFAM**ily" to come and take us home.

The Barber Family.

Barber's Tobacconists in Kirkgate is the oldest family run business in the town. James Barber, the present owner, has traced his family tree back to Sampson Barber who was born in Otley in 1685. The family has lived in the town ever since.

James's great grandfather Joseph, founded the business in his early twenties, opening a the shop with a factory at the rear in Kirkgate. At the same time he obtained two plantations in North Carolina at Rocky Mount and Providence, Kentucky, acquired by dispensation from the US government to take over non-productive, unoccupied land.

During his lifetime Joseph crossed the Atlantic over seventy times and on an early voyage, met a gentleman from Brooklyn. Concerned that Joseph, only in his twenties, was travelling alone, the gentlemen told him if he was ever in trouble, he must get in touch. This was the start of a friendship which was to help Joseph in years to come.

Joseph employed black labour on his plantations which came to the attention of the Klu Klux Klan. They warned Joseph that he should not to pay 'blacks' wages, and that they would return if he continued to pay his black workers. The Klan knew that Joe had to continue to work the land and keep it productive in order to keep it, so when he ignored their demands they destroyed his crops and possessions. After a refusal from a bank in Otley for a loan to replant his tobacco, he turned to his friend from Brooklyn who kept his promise and lent him money.

Joseph kept an all-night vigil at the plantations and when the Klan returned he shot nineteen of them, killing at least three. Fearing for his life he left the South for good,

leaving his younger brother to run the plantation. He returned to the States occasionally, meeting his brother in Brooklyn to discuss the running of the plantations, but he never ventured back to the Deep South.

After Joseph's death in 1912 the business was taken over by his son, Fred, who ran the business and factory until it burned to the ground in 1938. The property was then sold to FW Woolworth.

Fred's sons, Fred junior and Jack opened a small shop at number 22 Kirkgate. Fred junior retired in the 1960's and Jack, (James's father), moved the business across the road to number 33 Kirkgate where it is situated today.

James Barber now runs the shop, doing much of his business through the Internet. He is known throughout the world and the shop has won national awards. James was voted the Cigar Retailer of the Year (Northern Regional winner) and more recently, Pipe Retailer of the Year in the UK.

Dacres - an Old Established Otley Firm

The firm's founder John Dacre, was born in Bramhope in 1790, doing business as 'shoemaker and collector of taxes' from his home in Bramhope. The collector of taxes was an important person in those days being linked with the name of 'appraiser' Tax was often satisfied by a transfer of goods rather than cash, and the values had to be assessed.

The first office in Otley was opened in 1847 in Bondgate, at which time the firm was described as 'Auctioneer and Appraiser Northern Counties Association'. Otley was fast becoming a busy manufacturing as well as a market town and from 1850 the business was conducted in a house and shop in Northgate. When in 1860 John Dacre died he was succeeded by his son, also called John, who in 1866 moved to premises in the centre of the town in the yard behind Kirkgate.

In 1881 new offices were acquired in Station Road on the opposite corner to the present site and within five years a single storey block of offices sitting on the present site was purchased. This was subsequently replaced by the present building in the late 1930s. John Dacre junior, having taken over the business from his father when he died in 1860, was succeeded on his own death by his eldest son Charles Bentley Dacre, who apart from being a capable Auctioneer and Valuer, had a great interest in agriculture. His deep interest in livestock led him to start an auction mart which subsequently became the 'Otley Livestock Auction Mart' based on the east side of West Chevin Road which, according to an old calendar dated 1891, held out Dacre and Son as the originators of livestock sales in Wharfedale.

After Charles died in 1899, John William Dacre continued the practice taking into his partnership his sons and Brian and Maurice Dacre. Charles' other son, Charles Dacre, became a solicitor and joined his uncle Henry Dacre, who was articled to Thomas Constable of the Manor House, and was for some time Deputy Steward for the Manor of Otley. Brian and Maurice Dacre were sadly killed in the first world war and on the death of J W Dacre the firm was sold in 1926 to ASW Berry.

In 1932 the firm was purchased by Douglas Smallwood who took his partner William Horn Varley as a cattle man. The character of the practice however began to change to include the sales and lettings of all types of properties. The present offices were expanded in 1969 but since 1977 Dacre Son & Hartley has expanded its coverage of north and west Yorkshire, now having eighteen residential sales offices with two dedicated commercial offices in Leeds and Bradford.

The firm has had to move on the tide of technology with the reliance on information technology in every department of the firm.

Significant changes have taken place since the partnership was incorporated into a limited company in 1987. All the former partners continued with the firm except Andrew Hartley, who subsequently set up his own company, Andrew Hartley Fine Arts Limited.

Approaches in the 1980s by various financial institutions resulted in the business been acquired by Abbey National Estate Agents Limited, but not without strong representation from the Directors of Dacre Son & Hartley that the name of the firm should be retained. The wheel turned full circle and financial institutions became disillusioned with ventures into estate agency, and the opportunity to buy the company back occurred in 1995, when it returned to local ownership with Jim Horsley at Ilkley as chairman, and Martin Thompson at Otley as managing director.

The company's activities cover the whole of the United Kingdom on the commercial side, and it is involved in land development, planning issues, sale, valuation and management of both residential and commercial properties, and the valuation of plant and machinery primarily associated with the paper making industry. The profile of the business has changed dramatically since the early twentieth century, but contact with the traditional agricultural base of Dacre and Son is maintained through Dacre Son & Hartley's management of extensive estates of grouse moors and agricultural land.

It is a reflection of the town's tradition in the production of printing machinery that Dacre Son & Hartley currently prints all sales particulars for the company in a print room in its Otley offices and also produces a comprehensive guide covering the region. Computer networks ensure that the availability of any client's property is registered with each office and available on the internet.

Stationery Manufacturing – William Sinclair and Sons (Stationers) Limited

William Sinclair was born in Otley in 1815; the Sinclair family having moved to Otley from Pateley Bridge in 1779. At the age of 15 he was apprenticed as a printer and bookbinder to William Walker on Kirkgate. At the age of 22, shortly after serving his apprenticeship, he moved to Wetherby and in 1837, the year Queen Victoria acceded to the throne, founded the business of William Sinclair – Printer, Bookseller, Bookbinder and Stationer.

In 1854 he moved the business to premises in Westgate recently vacated by William Dawson where the first 'Wharfedale' printing press was built. His two sons, Jonathan and John William, took over the business following their father's death in 1865. Increased business demanded new premises and in 1884 they bought a field called Low Lycks on which to build a new factory. This is the present site in what is now North Street and Courthouse Street. The factory, known as Albert Works, was extended four times around the end of the nineteenth century and employed about 70 people.

As the twentieth century began the company had offices in London and Dublin It exported around the world, many goods starting their journey at Otley Railway Station: indeed some goods were still being taken to the station by horse and cart in the 1950s! The latter part of the twentieth century saw even greater expansion under the steward-ship of Jonathan's son, William Frederick Sinclair, his grandson, Michael Sinclair and also Cyril Moxon. To meet the increased demand there came new buildings in North Street and Courthouse Street and the purchase of the former Wharfedale Saw Mills from Peter Patrick. A major fire in 1979 destroyed part of the Patrick's site which was rebuilt over the ensuing years. By this time the factory had become known as Silvine Works, named after Sinclair's trade mark. In 1991, the Wharfedale Iron Works in Bremner Street were purchased for warehousing. There has been substantial investment in the lat-est automated machinery. The company currently employs over 200 persons, the pres-ent directors being Andrew Howard and Jonathan Medley (Michael Sinclair's sons-in-law) and David Moxon.

Products currently manufactured include refill pads, exercise books, duplicate books, scrap books, drawing books, notebooks, spiral notebooks, jotters, bound books, cloak-room tickets and personal stationery. Many of these are produced under the famous SIL-VINE brand name which was first used in 1901. Stationery is also produced under cus-tomers' own brand names. Customers include wholesale stationers, national retailers, commercial and contract stationers and educational supply organisations. Stationery is still exported to various countries.

Sinclair's is now one of Otley's oldest companies and still very much a family company. In addition to the Sinclair family, whose fifth generation now run it, many of the employees are from families whose parents, grand-parents, and great grand-parents also have worked for the company and contributed to its success over the years. But the com-pany does not rest on its history. It has achieved the national Quality Standard and recently was granted the Investors in People Award. Silvine products can be seen in many outlets and the company is one of the major stationery manufacturers in the country and the market leader in many areas.

The Legal Profession

Despite the vast increase in the population of Otley since the 1830s, there has been no increase in the numbers of solicitors, referred to until the mid 1850s as 'attorneys'. Many firms have practised in Otley but three who still remain have been established over one hundred years.

Made in Otley: The KB Special car was made in Otley around 1918 by King Brothers Motor and Aero Engineers of Cross Green

Once Upon A Vine

Chateau Otley? Yes, you may wonder – wine from Otley?   But yes, it's true, for hidden down the side of Dennison Hill just off Pool Road coming out of Otley, you will find Once Upon A Vine. Following a Canadian concept, where over 30% of their wine is produced locally in micro-wineries to avoid swingeing import duties, they have developed this idea and now produce quality wines to rival the best of those available from normal wine merchants.

The production method allows for the wine to be made virtually free of chemicals. Most commercial wines carry a fairly large sulphite content which contributes to those 'morning after' headaches, but not so in this case. Your only headache will be to choose which wine to order next.

At Once Upon A Vine the proprietor, Sheila Crowther, is now producing wines for customers in the same manner as the Canadians and, by following the rules laid down by HM Customs & Excise, can produce a top quality product at 'Duty Free' prices. Once Upon A Vine is happy for people to pop in for 'tastings' so you can try before you buy and at the same time they can explain the production process and how the system works.

They can also offer a personalised label service which is a great idea for celebrations such as weddings and anniversaries.

Brewery

Briscoe's Brewery is a unique micro-brewery owned and operated by Dr. Paul Briscoe, a PhD microbiologist who has been brewing quality 'full mash' beers at home for 20 years. Following redundancy from the chemical industry, Paul established the original brewery in November 1998 on a shoestring in the cellar of his red-brick semi-detached house in Ash Grove, Otley, using his long experience as a home brewer to devise novel but effective brewing plant from plastic buckets, watering cans and picnic coolers! The brew length at home was just one barrel (36 gallons/164 litres), making this one of the smallest commercial breweries in Britain. Despite the unusual equipment and lack of space, the beers quickly gained a fine reputation for their character and flavour and demand soon outstripped supply. Trevor Wallis and Judith Walker at the Bowling Green, the brewery's main outlet, came to the rescue and a new three barrel brewery was built in an outhouse at the rear of the pub. This new brewery, launched in March 2000, now produces quality cask ales for the free trade, beer festivals and public sale. All of the beers are naturally-conditioned 'real ales' to bring out the true flavour and character of the ingredients. To date the brewery has produced over 25 different beers, each with its own individual character. Brewery visits are welcomed by prior arrangement.

Time – Man – Rocks - Earth

Assume one second to be a lifetime of 70 years. If the birth of Christ is treated as taking place in the opening second of New Year's day we are at present not even half a minute into the New Year.

The last Ice Age was 6.5 minutes ago and only 8.5 minutes ago man was making his way into Europe.

Otley was being formed 300 million years ago approximately 10th November 'last year' when reptiles were just evolving in the pattern of life. It was back in August when crustacea appeared to be leaving us with our ancient fossils (not those found in Yorkshire).

By 1st January a year ago we have only gone back 2,000 million years.

We have to go back another year again to get a date for the oldest known rocks and back to the summer of that year for the origin of our planet. That is a long, long time ago, in fact some 145 thousand million million seconds or 207 million million lifetimes.

Population

In 827 AD the Manor of Otley covered a large but fluctuating area. By the time of the Doomsday survey of 1086 it included the following townships: Middleton, Denton, Clifton, Farnley, Timble, Weston, Pool, Guiseley, Esholt, Hawksworth, Baildon, Menston, Burley and Ben Rhydding. In this large area only about 36 families lived representing a population of under 200, of these fewer than half would be living in the town of Otley. This represented a low ebb in Otley's fortunes as the area would not have recovered from William I's 'harrowing of the North' in 1068-69. The next 120 years were a period of growth and by the time of the 1307 *Extent* we are able to estimate the population of the town at about 600. Then followed a period of decline brought about by the Scottish raids, the Black Death, years of bad harvests and the Wars of the Roses. We have no idea what the population dropped to but

we do know from the 1672 Hearth Tax which listed 122 houses in Otley giving an estimated population of 580 that by that date the population had barely reached the 1307 figure. The eighteenth and nineteenth centuries were a period of steady growth of the town as the following figures show:

1720: (calculations from Parish Registers) Population 884
1811: (Baines Directory) 2,602 *1931:* 11,020 *1951:* 11,508 *1961:* 11,930 *1964:* 11,770 *1965:* 11,860 *1966:* 11,960 *1967:* 11,950 *1971:* 13,272 *2001:* 15,000.

Television

When I last wrote about the subject in 1977, *Emmerdale* and its cast were to be seen regularly in Otley or Hotton, as it is known in the series.

A great deal has changed in the past 25 years but still we see plenty of TV crews in the town. The area has been used for *How We Used To Live, Hadleigh, Raffles, Music from Harewood, Heartbeat* and more.

The factor that originally made our area suitable has not changed: a range of suitable locations near a production centre. What has changed dramatically is the equipment used. Gone are the days of big outside broadcast units that covered anything from major state occasions or sporting fixtures to location drama. The advent of the Betacam with its ability to record its own pictures and small size meant that video location work could be done, on the format of film technique but with the benefits of video. Instead of large complex and costly mobile studio rooms, the recorded content is assembled in electronic editing suites back at base. It was said that this would get rid of the travelling circus but for those who see the current production in action, you might well not see much change!

In 2002 we had an Otley family starring on national TV as they re-lived the life in London during the blitz of 1940. In fact, the life I experienced as a child in London!

Otley Show

The farmers around Otley in the late 1700s were keen to apply developments in agriculture taking place elsewhere in the UK. Certainly in 1796 a competition for various livestock classes was conducted in the yard of the Royal White Horse, now Barclays Bank plc. The Show acted as a focus for the local farming community to promote and encourage improvements in livestock breeding and in the early days of Otley Show, substantial sums of money were placed as wagers.

In 1804 Jones Whitaker of Burley in Wharfedale and the Reverend Armitage Rhodes of Horsforth visited William Coke of Norfolk to see his renowned stock. On their return and with support from Sir Henry Carr Ibbetson of Denton Park, a society was formed for the encouragement and improvement of agriculture.

Therefore in 1806 the Wharfedale Agricultural Society was formed to organise the Shows. Originally two shows per year were held, one at Easter and one in the late

Autumn. The Society not only regulated the shows but purchased agricultural implements for the local farming community to conduct trials.

The objectives of the Society still remain the same, to encourage and promote new farming methods and techniques, whilst maintaining and supporting the traditions of its former years for the farming and agricultural sectors.

The Otley Show is held usually on the third Saturday of May and is the first major agricultural show of the season. It is thought to be the oldest one-day show in the country. It attracts an average of 15,000 visitors and is considered by many exhibitors as a 'try out' for the season, hence attracting excellent quality stock entries, providing more than nine hours' continuous entertainment and attracting in excess of 3,000 exhibits.

2001 saw the cancellation of Otley Show due to Foot and Mouth disease and large losses were incurred but the enthusiasm and commitment by the organisers and volunteers will ensure that the Show continues to thrive in the coming years.

Otley Carnival

Otley Carnival is the successor to the Otley Friendly Societies Gala of the early part of the last century.

The Carnival in its present form has been running since 1983, and it has become one of the most popular events in the town's calendar, attracting crowds of 30,000 or more. There are about 30 floats and walking groups and around ten marching bands in the Parade. Many charity and business stalls, children's rides and games compliment the crowning of the Queen on the Carnival field.

Between 1983 and the present, the Carnival has been able to give to Otley based charities and organisations between £50,000 and £55,000 in support of their various projects In addition, charity stalls on the field have raised in excess of £60,000.

It all makes for a fun-filled day for the entire community, but is of course mainly a children's day.

Victorian Fayre

Since 1985 there has been a Christmas Fayre and associated street market in Otley. It is usually held on the first Friday in December. The first Fayre was organised by the Chamber of Commerce as a commercial event. In 1987 it was decided that any surplus funds raised by the Fayre would be donated to a children's charity, one that might benefit an Otley child. During the following eight years over £31,000 was raised for children's charities.

In 1995 it was decided to include local charitable organisations that catered for the needs of adults as well as children. Since then a further £28,000 has been handed over to charities.

The Fayre is organised by a small, dedicated team of local people. Its purpose is to give people in the area an entertaining day, promote Otley and support local business by attracting a large number of visitors.

During the day local schools sing carols throughout the town centre. During the evening the main roads in the middle of the town are closed. There are children's rides and amusements, street organs, a miniature railway, Morris dancers, choirs and other events. In addition to the normal daytime market there is a special evening street market with charity stalls and specialist traders.

Opposite: 2nd Otley Scouts "Thomas the Tank Engine" float cleverly built around a Land Rover.

Right: Wilkinson Butchers

Otley Folk Festival

Otley Folk Festival was conceived in the upper room of the Yeoman public house in 1991 and was born on 18th September 1992. Artists appearing were regulars from the Otley Folk Club plus a smattering of musicians from folk's gallery of fame. Only five venues were used including two pubs, a total of only twelve events over the whole weekend, culminating in a massively overpopulated concern in the Red Lion on Sunday night.

Ten years later the attendance figures are believed to be 1,000 people per day going to 50 different events, to be entertained by local, national and internationally known artists, plus workshops and street entertainment.

The aim of the festival is to provide a weekend of varied entertainment for the benefit of the residents and traders of Otley and also to give excellent value for money to visitors from all parts of the country.

Town Cycle Race

Otley Cycle Club hosts and organises several prestigious events in the cycling calendar including the Town Centre Road Race run in early August from the late 1980s. This event always draws a high profile entry from some of the country's top cyclists such as local Olympian Jon Clay, members of the Lynda McCartney and Team England racing teams together with elite riders from Otley Cycle Club and clubs from across the country.

Otley Green Fair

Otley Green Fair is a non-profit making event organised by a group to promote awareness of environmental and ethical issues. It is a one day, free entry, family oriented event with stalls, practical sessions, good food and entertainments for all.

Originally held in the 1980s the Green Fair was restarted as a regular event in the early 90s. It has now become a regular biennial event with the most recent taking place in March 2001.

Cycle Hill Climb

The October Hill Climb, started in 1929 and featuring a lung-bursting climb up Norwood Edge and Otley Chevin, is another event that draws the crowds and some of the hard men of cycling.

Ten Mile Run

Otley Athletics Club's premier event run each May from Otley Maypole to Pool, Leathley, Farnley and back to Otley Rugby Club. It attracts top-class runners with a field of over 200 competitors.

Wharfedale FM

In December 2000 Wharfedale FM went on the air for the first time. Broadcasting from the offices of the Wharfedale and Airedale Observer, the station was operated by a number of volunteers and broadcast from 7.00am to 11.00pm for nine days.

The aim of the station was to provide good local community radio irrespective of colour, disability or political persuasion. It is hoped, if funding is found, that further broadcasts will be made.

Right: Nigel Francis of Wharfedale FM

Otley Vintage Transport Extravaganza

The Otley Vintage Transport Extravaganza was started in 1996. Held on the Bridge End Auction Mart site, the first rally attracted almost 100 vehicles, these ranging from 1920 cars to 1970s articulated tractor units. For the past four years the rally has been held at Knotford Nook, Pool Road, Otley, and nowadays attracts in the region of 200 vehicles. Unfortunately, in the year 2001 due to the foot and mouth restrictions the event was cancelled. Normally the event is held on the first Sunday in September and attracts a crowd of around 5,000 people.

Otley Swimming Club Annual River Race

The annual River Race is held on the second or third Wednesday in July. This event, which started in 1914, is swum over 440 yards of the River Wharfe, finishing in Wharfemeadows Park. There are trophies for the first three male and female swimmers and also for the youngest swimmer. One of the youngest competitors was Elena Arter when she was aged six, who later swam for UK in the Olympics.

Micro Triathlon

An Otley Sports Council event for children from 8 to 12 years old. It is a small-scale event comprising swim-run-cycle. Originally held using River and Wharfemeadows, it has now moved to the grounds and pool of Prince Henry's Grammar School. We hope that another Otley youngster may one day make the British Olympic Team, as Richard Allen did in Sydney 2000.

Otley Walking Festival 2002

The Otley Walking Festival is organised by the Otley Town Partnership in association with other organisations and individuals. The first Otley Walking Festival was held in Millennium Year 2000 and is now an annual event. Over 1,000 people enjoy the extensive choice of guided walks and events during the Festival. Walks vary from short strolls to challenging moorland hikes, from town centre to beautiful countryside and from dawn chorus to midnight hikes. Special features of the Otley Walking Festival are the Chevin access walks with electric scooters, and the guided walks for the blind and partially sighted. Something for everyone to enjoy!

Scout Torch Race

A relay race of ten runners, with teams drawn from any of the Scout groups in the district.

The race runs from the Jubilee Clock to the summit of the Chevin. The Sam Ives torch was carried in 1935 to light the beacon and this tradition has carried on ever since but using a baton, and celebrated with the race in May each year.

Lapsed Events

River Festivals

Scouts revived the tradition of river festivals for the 1977 Jubilee. This was repeated in 1990 – 1996 by a consortium of Rotary Chevin, the Sports Council and the Tourism Committee. They were very successful: drawing huge crowds and raising thousands of pounds for local charities. They ceased to continue partly because large numbers of helpers were required to stage the event and also because insurance costs were high.

Chevin Fell Race

A race from the Jubilee Clock to the top of Chevin and back organised by the Chamber of Trade. The races took place in the late 1980s.

Opposite: Made in Otley - Yellow Submarine built for wreck exploration now used as a Carnival float.

National Triathlons

A series of Grand Prix events that involved a 1,500m swim down the Wharfe, a 45km cycle ride of two circuits over Norwood Edge and Timble followed by a 6km run through Farnley Estate that were organised by Leeds Leisure Services and Otley Sports Council in 1986, 87, 88 and 89.

Local GP Dr Nick Allen and Jonathon Sedgewick figured strongly in these events.

Arts Festivals

A series of Arts Festivals were organised by D Cattanach from 1986 – 1996. These were followed by some outdoor events in Wharfemeadows Park in 1997 – 1999.

Stretcher Race

Formerly organised by Otley Round Table the races involved teams carrying a member and visiting many pubs in town for obligatory refreshment en route.

Review

Millennium Celebrations

Year 2000 got off to a stunning start in Otley with the Millennium Bonfire celebrations at Surprise View on the Chevin. Months of preparation and excellent teamwork by a group of willing volunteers, along with good weather, made the event one which will not easily be forgotten. About 2,000 people made their way to the top of the Chevin to enjoy the magnificent bonfire and a view of the fireworks being set off in the valleys like a carpet of multi-coloured flowers.

During the months that followed, the Otley Alternative Domesday Book brought together a special collection of creative work made by people of all ages, to provide a 'snapshot of Otley in the year 2000' for future generations. A grant from the Family

Learning Millennium Awards enabled a professional artist and photographer to hold workshops for over 700 adults and children in all kinds of creative and artistic work. An eager group of volunteers received training in assisting both artists and participants in the workshops. An exhibition of the extraordinarily diverse, beautiful and fantastic contributions from groups, schools and individuals was held at the Civic Centre in June 2000 for six days and visited by over 1,500 people, including children from all the Otley schools. The finished 'Book', large perspex boxes with samples of all the contributions from 'A Day in My Life' diaries to images of local shops, bright ceramic tiles and wall hangings featuring people's favourite hobbies - is available for loan.

The Tower, the Otley Millennium Play, was a futuristic piece of music theatre written and composed by Michael Wood, a member of Otley Community Players. Funded by a 'Millennium Awards for All' grant, enabled workshops in drama, music, dance, costume, props and mask making to be held in the nine months leading up to the performances. An orchestra was specially created for the production, which involved over 100 adults and children, and took place on six nights in July 2000 at the Civic Centre.

Below:Prince Henry's Grammar School in the early eighties

1887 Golden Jubilee

On the occasion of Queen Victoria's Golden Jubilee, Otley was gaily decorated. A public tea was held for 2,500 children and teachers and commemorative medals were distributed. A tea and concert for the aged took place in the Mechanics Institute with 260 participants. The workhouse inmates had a special dinner, small gifts of tobacco, sweets and the like, were handed out and an open-air concert was held. There was a gala in Westbourne Park featuring a greasy pole, old English games, hot air balloons, etc. There was a firework display and a torchlight procession afterwards by the Otley Fire Brigade. The Beacon Fire was visible until 2am.

All these celebrations were at a modest cost: Teas £100, Medals £60, Band £7, and Ringers £5, Total £172. The Gala Committee had a budget of £30 of which they spent £22.10s.0d.

The Jubilee Clock

During March 1887 a committee was formed to organise the celebrations for the Queen's Golden Jubilee. There was a large attendance at the first meeting of the committee and all the gentlemen present promised amounts to the fund. The town was divided into districts and collectors appointed.

The objects of the fund were: a Jubilee Cottage Hospital, a Public Recreation Ground, and another at the discretion of the Committee. The total named for these objects was £1,400. During the early part of May it was decided that the plans for the cottage hospital and recreation ground would have to be abandoned, the amounts promised not being sufficient to carry out either of them. The subscribers would be asked to give their amounts to a newer and smaller scheme:

(1) The erection of a combined illuminated clock tower, a drinking fountain and a trough for animals, to be placed in a central position in the town.
(2) A children's gala. A public tea for 2,500 children and teachers. A meat tea for the aged, to the number of 250, followed by a concert by the Orchestral Society.
(3) The distribution of 2,500 commemorative medals, 1.75 inches in diameter, a portrait of the Queen on one side, the Otley coat of arms on the other and the words 'Otley Commemoration'. It was stated that 'As a souvenir these will be worth preserving, being the very best that are procurable. About 100 in silk-lined cases will be available for sale, the cost probably being 1s each'.

Later in the month the idea of the clock was scrapped, this being thought to be unnecessary and the number of medals was increased to 3,000. By July, the committee had to think again. After the June Jubilee Celebrations a balance of £125 remained – not sufficient for an ornamental drinking fountain for human beings and animals. It was then determined to erect an illuminated clock in the Market Place, and to place a number of seats by the side of the most frequented walks in Otley.

When accounts were passed for payment in November for 25 seats there was £87 left. A design for a stone clock tower, to carry a 3 feet diameter set of four illuminated dials was submitted by Mr A Marshall. The total height of the tower would be 31 feet. The cost would be close on £150 and a further effort to raise £60 or more was requested by the committee. During December a cheque for £20 was received from Mr J Barran MP and a note saying 'I think the memorial will be both useful and appropriate'. The contract was accepted though a further £20 was still needed.

In 1888, donations continued to come in and the clock tower was under construction. At a meeting of the Jubilee Committee in May, an objection was made to the site. The objector offered £10 to the fund if the tower was moved; the committee visited the site but decided 'they liked it even better where it was' and decided to complete the building on their chosen site. The work of the committee terminated on Saturday 21 June 1888, when the ceremony of starting the clock took place. The clock 'was set a-wagging' at 4 o'clock in the afternoon by five year old Harold, son of Mr T A Duncan. He doffed his cap and waved it in the air, calling for 'three cheers for the Queen'. Mr Duncan then addressed the assembly, followed by Mr Jas Johnston, who on behalf of the Jubilee Committee, presented the tower, clock and the Jubilee seats to the Chairman of the Local Board in trust for the people of Otley.

The clock tower was built by Mr W Maston, from a drawing by Mr Alfred Marshall at a total cost of £180. The painting and gilding were done free by Mr H Pullan of Brunswick Villa, Otley and his son, Mr James Pullan of Bradford.

Jubilees and Coronations

1887: Queen Victoria's Golden Jubilee

1897: Queen Victoria's Diamond Jubilee. Singing and dancing in Otley town centre until 1:00 am. Barker's Leather Works strung 14 hides across the street, each bearing a letter, which spelt out the message 'Empress of India'.

1902: Coronation of Edward VI. Celebrations started at 6:00am with a peal of bells from the parish church and didn't stop until 1:00am the following day. Torchlight procession led by a band to a bonfire in Beacon Field. Royal salute of rockets from parish church tower at 10:45 pm.

1911: Coronation of George V. Otley had three days of celebrations and according to press reports: "Few towns of similar size could boast such an exhaustive programme thanks to the munificence of Colonel Dawson of Ashfield House who decided that the young and old of Otley should right royally celebrate. He handed over the sum of £250 to defray the whole cost of entertainment.

1935: Silver Jubilee of George V. Free cinema entertainment at Beech Hill Cinema, but even more watched Enid and Lulu; Featherstone's dancing girls. 8:00pm: Dancing to a band in the square. 10:00 pm: Beacon lit on Chevin.

1937: Coronation of George VI. Three days of festivities again. The middle day, Monday, was the big day, and every child at school in the town received a souvenir spoon and mug from the Council. They got a free cinema show too. At noon there was a royal salute of 31 guns. The Chevin Beacon burned at 10:10 pm again thanks to a relay of Boy Scouts.

1952: Coronation of Queen Elizabeth II. As well as all the usual merry-making, *'A Pageant of Otley'* was performed by the Otley Little Theatre in the Mechanics Hall. This was a dramatised account of the major incidents in the history of the town.

Made in Otley: Electric train made in 1927 by Charles Conradi, the grandfather of Mervyn Lister. Its use was to take artillerymen to the guns on a branch line to Essex.

The Sam Ives Torch

The late Sam Ives made a Jubilee Torch for the Silver Jubilee on 6 May 1935. This was made of brass and carried by the Boy Scouts of Otley from the Jubilee Clock to the summit of the Chevin. It was used to light the Beacon on Surprise View which was one of a chain throughout Britain to celebrate the Silver Jubilee of King George V and Queen Mary.

After the Celebrations the Torch was presented to the Scouts of Otley, and on the first Friday of May each year the Scouts hold a relay race from the Jubilee Clock to a flagpole placed on the site of the original Beacon, the teams consisting of ten Scouts under the age of sixteen. The winning Troop holds the Torch for one year. The Sam Ives Torch was brought out again on 6 June 1977 to light the Beacon to celebrate the Silver Jubilee of Queen Elizabeth II and Prince Philip.

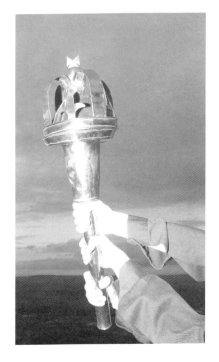

Looking back through the local paper archives for 1935, the year of King George V Silver Jubilee

JANUARY: We have an interesting contrast as a result of Otley being a conservation area. In 1935 storm damage resulted in three tons of masonry falling from Helliwell's shop (Boots) in Market Place. Result – a flat roof. The council decided by five votes to four to allow Sunday boating.

FEBRUARY: The great flood after a night of heavy wind and rain, floods were highest for 52 years. 50 houses marooned, river ten feet above normal. Otley Council accepted a free gift of fixtures of swing in Wharfemeadows park play ground.

MARCH: rate increase throughout the district. Otley rate up by 1s 2d to 14s 8d in pound. Garnett's went public; 30 mph speed limit introduced; Council installed three Belisha beacons.

APRIL: Easter holiday – variable weather, gloomy Good Friday, plenty of sunshine on the Monday.

MAY: Jubilee month events in other section. Heavy snow 16 May, 12 inches at Ilkley weather station. Otley Show record-breaking attendance of 4,132, yet made a loss of £8. Party of 570 people went on Wharfedale Observer chartered train to Edinburgh.

JUNE: Local Authority changes. Failure to establish a new, large area of Otley, Menston, Burley, Ilkley, due to County opposition. I wonder how Otley would have developed had that occured? New cattle market built north of the river, despite having been washed away in the flood of February – cost £7,000. Otley Swimming Club petitioned Ministry of Health about condition of Wharfemeadows pool.

JULY: Fine weather and talk of midnight bathing in the Wharfe. Otley Rugby Club bought new stand to seat 1,100 – cost £500. P R T Garnett achieved top score in national shooting competition.

AUGUST: Must have had a good spell of weather as cricket interfered with for first time in the season. Otley children camp at Skyreholm. 100 acres of Blubberhouses Moor on fire. Queen passed through on her way to Bolton Abbey.

SEPTEMBER: Twelve clubs of Wharfedale and Airedale section of Yorkshire Cricket Council resigned and formed Wharfedale and Airedale cricket league. Petition for traffic lights at Dyneley Arms due to many accidents. General Eva Booth passed through Otley – held up by large crowds.

OCTOBER: Otley Swimming Club again press for action on swimming pool. Otley and District Round Table received its Charter.

NOVEMBER: General Election on 14th. Wet night for bonfires.

DECEMBER: Council approve £2,000 for improvements to Wharfemeadows pool including re-tiling and installing filtration plant for water. Traffic lights installed at Dyneley Arms. A record 442 students at Prince Henry's Grammar School compared with 126 in 1918 when the school re-opened. First snow of the season on 14th – skating possible on local lakes and dams. Newall School built for 200 children at a cost of £4,200.

1952 – 2002 Local Events

Looking back over the last fifty years in Otley, here is a very condensed and abbreviated account of some of the interesting events that have taken place. It all began in 1952 with the death of the King. 9 February Cllr Harry Spence read a Proclamation from the flag-draped balcony of the Royal White Horse Hotel to a stilled Otley, after which the Salvation Army Band played the National Anthem, and three cheers were given for the Queen. 15 February: the funeral brought Otley to a standstill. Parish Church bell tolled 56 times and a memorial service was held.

May: Dedication of the new Civic Regalia obtained by public subscription, and the patent of arms obtained by the Council costing 100 guineas. The 145th Otley Show saw 1,000th member enrolled. The West Riding County Council announced development plans for Otley schools. Otley Photographic Society obtained 200-year-old loving cup to be awarded for competition results. Otley Hospital Board established a ward for treatment of old people. Len Hutton chief guest at Dawson Payne & Elliott's annual sports club dinner. Second year DP&E won Challenge Cup, and soccer Championship League for second time in three years. Phillip Whitehead won Yorkshire's hardest cycling event, a federation twelve-hour time trial. Alfred Myers awarded MBE in New Year's Honours List. Otley Girl Guides celebrated 25th birthday.

1953: To mark Coronation year, another badge of office to be worn by the Chairman's Lady was presented to the Council. Weston Lane Primary School costing £56,000 opened to accommodate 320 children. Over £2,600 was raised for renovation and decoration of the Methodist Church. Otley Little Theatre put on 'Pageant of Otley' from historic research and writing of Fred Morrell and Eric Cowling. M Bancroft and Mrs E Bancroft won Wharfedale Tennis League Cup and league mixed doubles. Otley Mills won Wharfedale League Bowls Championship. New club formed for business and professional women. First visit to town by Chancellor of Exchequer, Mr R A Butler. Founder member of Otley Retail Butchers' Association, Mr J B Shaw, retired after 65 years in the trade. Mr H M Bradley awarded British Legion's highest award certificate of merit. Second Otley Boy Scouts, believed to be one of the oldest groups in the country, celebrated their 40th birthday. Otley Swimming Club celebrated its golden jubilee.

1954: Otley and Wharfedale Mission closed down after 76 years of service and witness. Otley Little Theatre showed great concern over impact of television upon their audiences. Wharfe was completely frozen over in February. Keys of 56 Weston Drive, 1,000th Otley Council house, were handed over by Cllr Mrs I Wilkinson. Second Otley Scout Master, Owen Holmes, visited London to receive Scouting's highest honour from the Chief Scout in recognition of 41 years' service. Sporting history made by DP&E being first Otley team to win the County Cup. Two old-established businesses announced their closure: J W Helliwell Ltd, founded over 70 years ago and spanning three generations, and W Robinson Ltd founded in Boroughgate in 1885. Otley Grammar School welcomed 1,200 visitors to indoor garden party. Otley Rugby Club opened new Clubhouse at Cross Green Ground. Otley DP&E Cricket team won championship of Airedale and Wharfedale Senior League. Otley Congregational Church celebrated 133rd Anniversary. Otley Westgate School installed electric lighting system.

1955: Scholars at Weston Lane School presented chronicle play titled *'God and Mankind'*, written by Mr V Shaw, assistant schoolmaster. Otley Methodists celebrated jubilee of Wesley Hall opened in 1905. May was a busy month with Otley Show, a General election, Local Urban, Rural and Parish Council Elections. Over 300 guides and brownies from Wharfedale attended a service at Otley to mark Empire Youth Sunday. June marked 75th Anniversary of first Observer dated 14 June 1880. At P Garnett & Son the main engine, which had supplied the power since 1924, was shut down and replaced by new plant. Otley firms exhibited at Printers Machinery Exhibition in London. DP&E had 14 machines on show, Waite & Saville Ltd, 7. Largest budgerigar and foreign bird show ever held in Otley had 509 entries. Nurse Ruth Adams retired after 23 years' service as Health Visitor in Otley.

1956: Otley & District Little Theatre's 50th show. Very severe March gales damaged hundreds of houses and uprooted trees, leaving worst trail of destruction in living memory. Otley AFC obtained two acres of derelict land (old show field), and made it into a playing area and established a well-appointed dressing room. Otley & District Round Table raised £73 for a boys' holiday camp and communal service activities. Film star, Miss Joan Rice, visited Otley in connection with the effort. Otley Young Conservatives had 50 entries for annual Regatta on the Wharfe. Otley Golf Club celebrated its Golden Jubilee. 600 people attended Rugby Club on bonfire night for fireworks display.

1957: Otley Council accepted Mechanics Institute's offer of their building as gift to town. Tenth annual reunion of Otley Air Training Corps squadron. April - Otley Bridge opened to two-way traffic. 150th Otley Show graced by Princess Royal who made a tour of the showground. Sunniest June for 17 years - 385.9 hours of sunshine. Otley's water supply reduced to 70 days. Situation worse than drought years 1911 and 1921. Jamaican scouts, over for Jamboree, were guests of Otley scouts for five days. Sponsored by Otley Rotary Club and supported by local industries and trades people, 12,000 people visited 'Otley Can Make It' exhibition staged in Mechanics Institute. Imperial Service Medal awarded to Mr Foster for service during his 38 years as postman. Salvation Army held evangelistic campaign. Hugh Gaitskill visited Otley. Speech Day at Prince Henry's Grammar School celebrated 250th Anniversary of granting of school's charter.

1958: A party of Japanese visitors attended meeting at Otley Council. Otley RUFC celebrated its Golden Jubilee attended by 100 men who had at some stage played for the club over the last 50 years. Otley Rotary Club celebrated 25th Anniversary. Otley Secondary School won the Nunns Cup in the Airedale and Wharfedale Schools' Sports Association.

1959: - Otley Council initiated steps to try to improve television reception in the town. Otley Round Table celebrated 25th Anniversary. Around 50 married couples stood hand in hand at a marriage re-union service in the Parish Church. Otley Council announced first steps to form a museum. Mr Richard Pratt retired from Prince Henry's after 41 years. Balloon released during Otley Shopping Week travelled 125 miles to Droitwich. Meeting of local organisations decided Otley should twin with a town in France. Committee to select a suitable town. September - continuing drought. Otley clamped down on all water use. Station Road Tannery 'well' opened up and contributed 60,000 gallons a day. Library moved to present premises with stock of 12,000 books. Nurse Ruth Pollard received Cazenove Medal from Queen for nursing. Cllr Mrs Dorothy Lambert expelled from Otley Labour Party. Continued as Independent for the rest of her term of office. DP&E introduced a sheet-fed rotary letterpress which put them at forefront of British developments in this field. Otley one of the places suggested for Leeds overspill. Otley put in a ten-mile foot and mouth restricted area.

1960: GCE Course introduced at Otley Secondary School. Otley & District Round Table held 25th Anniversary in February. Otley Council Meeting major bombshell decision to increase council house rents by 9d per week. Rates fixed at 23s 8d in the pound, the highest in the history of the town. £190 included in estimates for next year for the replacement of Otley's rotting maypole. Replaced by a steel structure. 'Maggie,' the Moor Drive pet magpie, was found to be pecking babies in prams and the RSPCA was called to remove it. Post Box No 551 stolen from West Chevin Road was retrieved from Menston Quarry. Over 200 young Otley swimmers queued outside gate of Wharfemeadows swimming pool at the start of the season. Otley Parish Church Troop scout won 'Sam Ives' Trophy for Torch Race. Construction of swimming pool commenced at Weston Lane School. August aerial survey showed Otley to be major black spot for traffic hold-up in whole of county. Over 3,500 people attended Wharfemeadows swimming pool during August holiday. Old Lodging House demolished in Bondgate to improve bend in road. Fire damaged large hall in Mechanics Institute putting ballroom out of action. Fire damaged pavilion of Otley Wesley C C. Kirkgate Picture House to be converted into a supermarket. Otley firemen 'syndicate' won first dividend of over £1,300 on Football Pools.

1961: Street lighting criticised in Leeds Road after fatal accident. Fire caused extensive damage at Mounsey's Stationers shop in Kirkgate. 459 people watched free-style wrestling for first time in Otley at the Mechanics Institute. Many people had to be turned away. 150th Anniversary of Wm Walker & Sons Ltd with presentations for 30 or more years' service. 100-year-old organ rebuilt for £1,800; used for first time in Otley Catholic Church. Otley forestry plantation in Danefield won Yorkshire Show Bronze Medal. Otley Swimming Club opened by Channel swimmer Miss Dorothy Perkins (19). Eleven Otley Parish Church scouts went on Continental camping holiday visiting five countries and covering 2,500 miles. Model railway exhibition in Library attracted good deal of interest.

1962: Doctors worked non-stop for almost 15 hours following confirmed case of smallpox. Shoppers queued two hours for opening of Meadow Dairy Supermarket in Kirkgate. 12 February gale left trail of havoc, returning on the 15th when for first time in 30 years there was no market. Mr Vernon Barritt appeared on television and explained idea of school system consisting of four terms instead of three. New 75 feet maypole was erected at cost of nearly £300. First 'no waiting' area came into force in Boroughgate.

Ripon Divisional Headquarters of Liberal Party opened in Boroughgate. Mr E C Biss, Editor of the *Wharfedale & Airedale Observer* described Otley as a 'happy, homely and friendly town' in BBC's *'Talk in Focus.'* In June Mr Biss retired after 56 years, 34 years as Editor. Otley Magistrates heard first summonses from speed checks by radar equipment. Twin town links established with Montereau, France, largely through efforts of Mr N Bousefield, Grammar School Headmaster. 25 pupils from Grammar School left for ten-day skiing holiday in Austria. A machine from DP&E printed 224-page newspaper in Orense, Spain. Representatives from Otley attended.

1963: David Wilkinson (9) was rescued by Christopher Haigh (14) from ice-covered Wharfe. Biscuit factory of W Robinson (Otley) Ltd, Station Road closed. With 70 days' supply in the reservoirs, Rombalds Water Board appealed that water should be conserved. Wharfe froze over - animal lovers urged to feed swans and hack holes in river. Unemployment figures rose to 199 - 70 were unemployed because of bad weather. The cold icy weather persisted; local clubs had a sorry tale of unplayed fixtures. Thaw came in early March ending ten weeks of snow, frost and freezing winds. Authorisation given for erection of new Divisional Police Headquarters costing £70,000. Bruce Forsyth played round of golf at Otley. Mr William Whiteley of Pool opened Otley Aged People's Club in Cross Green. A dinner was held in Royal White Horse Hotel to commemorate Chippendale's birth in Otley. John K Slater, formerly of Otley, swam Lake Coniston in record time of 2 hours, 30 minutes and 40 seconds. Plans for £145,000 extension to Otley General Hospital were announced. Very wet June enabled water restrictions to be withdrawn. There followed the wettest Bank Holiday for more than 40 years. Cllr Swann said Otley would be killed by traffic congestion within next 10/20 years if nothing were done. End of 11-plus examinations in Wharfedale schools.

1964: Otley's own gas-producing unit became derelict with adoption of 'grid' system. Wharfedale Tennis Club wound up due to lack of support. Caledonian and Scottish Dancing Societies presented Scottish dancing on lawns of Ashfield Hotel. Otley Meals on Wheels Service began. Beech Hill Cinema to be closed for showing films but would be used for Bingo. £12,000 Youth Centre in grounds of Weston Lane School officially opened. Subscriber Trunk Dialling (STD) introduced to Otley. Record Christmas Mail at Post Office reached 313,000 items from 17 to 24 December.

1965: Remains of an iron sword found protruding from a bank to the north of Otley General Hospital were thought to date back to 1300. Last passenger train drew out of Otley railway station in snowstorm. Jack Charlton, Leeds United and England centre-half, presented trophies at final of Otley Weston Lane inter-street competition. Mr Derek Gill returned home to a civic reception after being first Otley man to swim Channel. W Ackroyd & Co Ltd, Otley Mills, celebrated 150th Anniversary. Under

Opposite: Made in Otley - A 124cc Puch engine Trials bike made in Leeds Road by Peter Edmondson during the sixties. This particular bike was extremely popular in the U.S.A.

terms of firearms amnesty, 77 weapons were surrendered; most in Yorkshire. November went out under snow followed by worst blizzard for years, then came rain and floods. Wharfe burst its banks and Otley was cut in two.

1966: Otley Golf Club opened its new £45,000 Clubhouse. Mr John Hannam won Producer's Award at Harrogate Drama Festival. Otley ambulance driver, Howard Green, awarded Royal Humane Society's Testimonial for attempt to rescue occupants of car submerged in river at Ilkley. Otley Chamber of Trade defeated Otley Council in annual bowls match in Wharfemeadows. New twin operating theatre suite and ward at Otley General Hospital opened costing £92,951. Otley had victory over Ilkley in BBC TV's 'It's a Knockout' but lost to Bridlington in county final. Harry Potter became Otley's first Traffic Warden. £306,350 new sewerage scheme approved by Council.

1967: The White House farm and outbuildings were purchased by Otley and District Scout crew for conference and camping centre. Thompsons beat Grove Hill 6 - 2 in final of workshops soccer competitions. French tricolour flag flew over Council Offices when 30 children from Montereau (twin town) were given civic reception. For third successive year Carlton Bell won river race. Lesley Aspinall (13) set up five new records at Swimming Gala. Jimmy Savile Guest of Honour at Otley's first Pop Civil Ball. Council Chairman, Ronnie Duncan, announced at the Ball that he had married Miss Henriette Stirk-Eugler earlier in the day. 'Save the Chevin' fund launched at public meeting to help pay legal costs for opposition of Chevin footpath.

1968: BBC Radio broadcast half an hour of hymns from Parish Church. 30 feet wooden cross placed on top of Chevin for Easter festivities. Percy Thrower opened Garden Centre on Pool Road. A freak July storm with torrential rain caused roads to run like rivers and brought traffic to a standstill. Human bones, believed to be of ancient origin, were found buried 14 feet deep on the North bank of the Wharfe. The lighting of a beacon on top of Chevin marked the start of Otley Youth Fiesta Week. 1,000 members enrolled in first week at new Weston Lane Social Club.

1969: The Bachelors opened new radio studio at Otley Hospital. Was announced that three shops and a house would be demolished for Fine Fare supermarket in Kirkgate. Hardboard figure of Christ appeared on Easter Cross in protest against Vietnam War. First tenants installed in British Legion ex-Servicemen's flats, West Busk Lane. Gunman snatched £6,500 after forcing driver of Securicor van to drive from hospital to Chevin. Runaway lorry careered down East Chevin Road leaving a 100 yards trail of havoc, damaging six parked vehicles. Miss Alice Bacon MP opened new clubroom at Otley Labour Party Headquarters. Concern expressed by Otley Road Safety Committee over hazards created by new access to Grammar School from Newall Carr Road. At Wharfedale Rural Council meeting it was decided that no objections in principle would be put forward against proposed extensions at Yeadon Airport. A display of exhibits found on site of the

'Manor House Dig' represented 1,000 years of Otley history.

1970: Dacre, Son & Hartley celebrated 150th Anniversary. 'Clean-up Campaign' set up for Otley. Yew Tree Farm, thought to date back 400 years, was converted into a public house. A small earthquake, which shook the North of England, was felt in Otley. Two young people completed an 80-hour disc jockey fund-raising marathon in broadcasting studio at hospital. The Royal Oak, believed to be Otley's second oldest Inn, was closed. HRH Prince Charles opened newly extended Prince Henry's Grammar School.

1971: Work started on laying 20cm North Sea Gas main through south of Otley. Concessionary bus fare tickets introduced for people aged 65 and over. Otley Show halted a series of losses. New television mast at Clifton became operational. Thomas Pickles (81) of Bridge Avenue achieved his lifetime ambition by publishing his story on the life of Thomas Chippendale. 100 pupils due to leave Grammar School were unable to find work. During renovation work at the Black Bull, workmen uncovered sixteenth century fireplace. Annual Flower Show, opened by Sir Malcolm Stoddart-Scott, celebrated its Golden Jubilee. New and revised Otley Draft Town Centre Map made available to the public. Otley residents were urged by Cllr Dr G Kirkland to write individually to Ministry of the Environment asking that some form of Council be retained in the town following Local Government reorganisation.

1972: Rev Ian James Langlands Browne of Bradford Road received MBE for his work for Yorkshire Safety Centre for the Construction Industry. A club to provide recreational facilities for all age groups was opened at Prince Henry's Grammar School. Crowds lined streets at military funeral of Private James A Lee of Ilkley Road who was killed in Ulster. John Churchman of Otley Cycle Club, was first Yorkshireman to win British Cycle Tourist Trial in its 21-year history. Cast iron crown of Jubilee Clock removed for safety reasons

1973: 'Flu' epidemic put pressure on hospital accommodation. BBC radio programme 'Down your Way' visited the town. Otley Council decided by eight votes to seven to make grant of £25,000 towards Grammar School swimming pool. Chairman of Council, Dr G Kirkland and his wife Dr J Kirkland, attended royal garden party at Buckingham Palace. In clean-up operation two lorry-loads of rubbish taken from riverbed. Otley firemen equipped with pocket alarm systems, replacing siren which had sounded for more than half a century.

1974: Otley Urban District council replaced by Otley Parish Council and Leeds City Council. Fire at Grammar School. Otley's marathon by-pass public enquiry, with 31 witnesses, lasted 50 hours spread over nine days. 80 tons of Canadian timber, valued £7,000, destroyed by fire at Otley Timber Yard. Mr Harold Walker celebrated 83rd birthday with swim at Aireborough baths. New Grammar School swimming pool opened. War Memorial at Grove Hill Park re-dedicated after vandalism.

1975: Reports of sheep rustling on moors above Otley. Loss of 27 Swaledale lambs and ewes valued £300. Complaints that hospital kitchen facilities were 'medieval' led to assurance that they would be improved or replaced. David McQueen retired after 25 years with Fire Brigade. Town Council discussed plans for recreation centre at Knotford Nook. Jimmy Savile signed autographs for 2nd Otley Scouts. Dinner held to celebrate Silver Jubilee of Otley Ladies Circle. Chancellor of the Exchequer, Mr Denis Healey, returned to Otley to present Labour Party's Award of Merit to Mrs Ethel Green of Bramhope. A silver trowel used by Mrs C H Dawson of Weston Hall to lay foundation stone of Otley Mechanics Institute in 1869, was presented to the Council by Col Dawson.

1976: January saw section of Courthouse Street cordoned off after high winds dislodged masonry from an old building. Public participation meeting on town's future. A group of planners faced barrage of questions, comments and criticism. A new geriatric unit was brought into use at the hospital. Dr Keith Hampson MP, planted tree from Otley Chevin in War Memorial garden. Otley officially declared to be an 'Outstanding Conservation Area of exceptional architectural and historic interest'. May electors registered their votes in first district town and parish council elections: Liberal 10, Conservative 5, Labour 0. Equipment was installed on river bank at Arthington to combat water shortage. There was a prolonged drought. Soaking rain and ankle-deep mud were the memories of Otley Show. Cllr Fred Atkinson, twice Chairman of the old Urban District Council, elected Town Mayor. Yorkshire Water Authority bought standpipes at the rate of 1,000 a week. Fortunately they were not needed in Otley. Annual River Race: men's winner - Andrew Dexter (15); women's - Allyson Armistead (13). Large crowd attended Otley Rugby Club's 'Donkey Derby' and Miss Susan Kay was 'Miss Otley RU.' August - The Fire Brigade turned out to a record 41 calls, mainly grass fires. Otley Sports and Leisure Exhibition attracted 2,000 visitors. Tributes paid to Nurse Ruth Adams at official opening of Adams Croft flats in Westgate. Vicar of Otley, Canon John Clayton, retired after 12 years in Otley. New vicar was Canon Desmond Max Kendrick. Rainfall in September totalled 8.83 inches (22cm) making it the wettest period for at least 70 years. Occupants of ten houses in Cambridge Drive spent a harassing weekend when a beck and culvert could not cope with torrential rain and caused flooding. Work started on 'facelift' to the Chevin. One of the jobs was to demolish Jenny's Cottage. Major projects were accepted for celebrations of the Queen's Silver Jubilee.

1977: Silver Jubilee fund launched, multitude of fund-raising events began including weighing the 1976/7 Town Mayor, Cllr Fred Atkinson in silver. Courthouse Street opened for Easter. New Draft Local Plan for Otley introduced by Leeds City Council. Cllr Richard Good invested as Town Mayor. One of his first duties was to attend Liberal Centenary celebrations at Civic Centre. Street Parties and jubilee beacon on the Chevin were some of the events held to celebrate the Royal Silver Jubilee. Weir strengthened with reinforced concrete. Jack D Simpson and Harold Walker were first appointed Honorary Citizens of Otley.

1978: Otley Woolpack Motor Club staged its first major Rally, with prizes and awards totalling nearly £500. Otley Rotary Club's 45th Charter Dinner was held at the Parkway Hotel, Bramhope.

1979: A 40 feet water well was discovered at Messrs G A Thackwrays on Bondgate during alterations. 1,500 people attended an Old English Sports Day held by Otley Rotary Club. Bramhope & Otley Round Tables held first Otley Stretcher Race. Telephone Exchange in Charles Street came into operation. A 14-strong team of locals from the Fountain Inn walked the three Yorkshire peaks to raise money for charity. New pelican crossing installed in Crossgate.

1980: Chamber of Trade launched first Chevin Fell Race. Otley was twinned with Montereau in France. Midland Bank moved from Kirkgate to new Crossgate premises. Wm Sinclair & Sons' new Courthouse Street warehouse was opened. Shops and cottages demolished to make way for Otley Building Society's extension.

1981: A few years late, viewing indicator at Surprise View was erected to mark Queen's Silver Jubilee. Courthouse Street's new parking area was opened. Extensive repair work began on Otley's Buttercross to renew roof and carry out other necessary repairs. It was announced that the 'Masons Arms' in Westgate would close its doors after 100 years. Schoolteacher, Betty Watson, retired after 27 years at All Saints Middle School. Otley - Pool Relief Road scheme given the axe. Street parties and barbecues were held to celebrate wedding of Prince Charles and Diana. Otley Golf Club left Bradford Union after 50 years' continuous membership. Last printing press came out of Crabtree Vickers' Workshop. Over three days, an estimated 1,200 people attended Otley Trades Exhibition sponsored by Otley Town Council. Wharfedale General Hospital Special Equipment Fund, set up in 1980 to raise funds to purchase specialised equipment for the hospital which would not otherwise be available from normal National Health channels, raised no less than £8,400 during its first year. Civic Centre keys were handed to Otley Town Council. Otley Building Society's extension opened. Go-ahead given for new low priced townhouses in Cambridge Street.

1982: Following a unique process developed by P Garnett & Son Ltd, 'Odasorb' insoles were now available at Stylo Barratt shoe shops. Otley divided in two as river burst its banks and possibly worst floods for 20 years. Seventeenth century Old Grammar School in Manor Square was put up for sale. Future of Otley Museum hung in the balance so steps were taken to form a fund-raising group under the name of 'Otley Museum Friends'. Otley Parish Church faced tower repairs which could cost as much as £23,000. Otley Unionist Club changed its name to Otley Conservative Club. Two-hour parking restrictions imposed on recently completed Courthouse Street car park. Sir Jimmy Savile took part in Otley's first half marathon. Go-ahead given for nature park to follow route of old railway line. Chevin Breakers CB (citizens band radio) Club presented cheques totalling £1,000 to Wheatfields Hospice and Otley Ladies Hospital Group. Otley Market Traders said re-arranged market to ease traffic problems was terrible. The merger of Otley Building Society with Skipton Building Society was approved by Otley Building Society's shareholders. Old Grammar School re-opened as new premises for Manor House China. Work on Otley Parish Church tower was completed.

1983: New lease of life given to Weston Lane pavilion following grant from Leeds City Council. Keep fit sessions on first floor at Otley Civic Centre caused noise problems for ground floor users. Otley Brass Band was in need of new premises and celebrated tenth anniversary. Twelve weeks old Benjamin Whitehead became a star as Matt and Dolly Skilbeck's newborn child in Yorkshire Television's soap 'Emmerdale.' Growing membership of Men's Forum brought problems. Due to waterlogged ground, Otley Show was cancelled at estimated loss of £4,000. Otley Carnival and Gala was revived. Margaret Thatcher visited Ogdens to test drive Albert, a remarkable device that stopped vehicles from reversing into solid objects. After several requests for a market on Good Fridays, the decision to change an 800-year-old tradition was put by Otley Council to Leeds City Council. Otley Athletics Club was formed and became affiliated to the Amateur Athletics Association. Phase one of Victorian shopping precinct in Westgate Arcade opened. First phase of Chevin Lodge on Yorkgate opened.

1984: Crabtree Vickers' Foundry closed with loss of 23 jobs. Otley bridge traffic lights caused chaos during footbridge repairs. Inglewood Children's Home in Bradford Road demolished to make way for by-pass. Otley Bellman, Alan Butler, took to the streets to renew an old tradition which had died out almost 70 years ago. First vacant Crabtree Vickers' buildings were demolished. Otley Library temporarily closed following collapse of exterior wall. Peter Lazarus, Under Secretary of State for the Department of Transport, opened Otley's £5.3m by-pass four months ahead of schedule. Michael Harrison, dentist, retired from practice after 32 years in Otley. Stephen and Frances Day were flown back to Otley from Brighton following bombing at The Grand Hotel. Piper Lane became a stream of cream after lorry spilt its load. Otley Athletic Club made good progress and topped 100 members. Otley's Market Place Co-operative shop closed after being on same site since early 1900s. Local opinion divided over decision to phase out £1 note next year. Jumbo jet took off from Leeds Bradford Airport for first time.

1985: Otley & District Photograph Society staged 40th annual exhibition. Market temporarily moved to Charles Street for 12 weeks during Market Place works. Hundreds of Prince Henry's Grammar School pupils declared lightning strike as supposed protest against industrial action taken by teachers in support of their pay claim. A British Airtours Tri-Star carrying 416 people plunged off end of runway at Leeds Bradford Airport. Parking on Otley's Market Place was made illegal, with exception of the disabled, following re-laying of setts. Otley Cycle Club's first Town Road Race was a success. New nightspot 'Moonlighters' opened behind Korks Wine Bar. Corner area of Bay Horse Passage given new look. Otley Small Business Forum formed to cater for the small trader, self-employed or almost anyone in business on their own account. New Inn Yard development scheme welcomed. Otley's first Victorian Fayre was huge success.

1986: Wesley Street closed in gas scare and businesses and homes had to be evacuated. Dr Jack Rhodes, who had been in general practice in Otley for 51 years, retired. Development began in June of the supermarket and housing on land between Westgate and Burras Lane, formerly the site of Crabtree Vickers. Gangs battled in town centre and 13 youths were arrested. John (Jack) and Elizabeth Taylor retired from The Fleece Hotel after more than 20 years as tenants. First of several Medieval Monday markets held in Market Place. Ten Otley Tetley Pubs changed their names to 'The Prince Andrew' for Royal Wedding Week to celebrate Prince Andrew's marriage to Sarah. Concorde flew into Leeds Bradford Airport for first time watched by a crowd of 70,000 people. First Otley Arts Festival. Former 'Fountain Inn' re-opened as the 'Yeoman' following extensive refurbishment. The Supermarket 'Presto' opened in Westgate/Burras Lane. Joanne Dexter, soprano, won Julie Andrews Award.

1987: Charles Street Medical Centre officially opened. AIDS shock at Otley Hospital when AIDS carrier was admitted. Gordon Longfield received safe driving award by Yorkshire Electricity Board. Otley Town Council 'go-ahead' for £300,000 land reclamation scheme to convert old sewage works into riverside parkland area. Statue to commemorate Otley cabinet maker, Thos Chippendale, was unveiled in Manor Square. Barclays Bank raided over one January weekend. Jack Lunn (Homes) Ltd. paid British Telecom over £2.5m for Kineholm site on which to build 76 homes. Mr Frank Lofthouse, veterinary surgeon, retired after practising in Otley since 1941. Ralph Bradley went on 440 mile run between Otley and Montereau. Otley Arts Club celebrated 40th birthday. Wm Sinclair & Sons Ltd celebrated 150th anniversary over several days, which included banquet for entire workforce. 200-strong protest rally marched through town in protest of Otley Hospital closure. Otley given tourist status by Leeds City Council so shops could open 18 Sundays during summer. Facelift for bus station unveiled. Mr & Mrs Tom Laycock retired after more than 50 years in Cross Green grocery shop. Larry Grayson visited Otley Parish Church to see friends Rob and Lesley Marshall. Vallances of Otley were included in a £10m deal between Vallances and Thorn EMI plc. Filming of 'How we used to Live' took place at William Walkers. Father Finn retired after 19 years as local Catholic Parish Priest. Pilot died in Chevin plane crash following loss of radio contact with Leeds Bradford Airport. Otley chartered accountant, Leslie Bray, retired after more than 30 years in town. 'Wharfedale & Airedale Observer' and 'Gazette' came under new management of Walker (Publishing) Ltd, a subsidiary of Walker Group Ltd. Double decker bus hit 'Needlecraft' and 'Wilkinsons' in Boroughgate. Driver and elderly passenger were taken to hospital but not detained. After six years of fundraising, St John Ambulance Brigade opened new Headquarters in Myerscroft costing around £40,000. Otley Parish Church Scouts and Guides' Parents Association started first annual Christmas postal deliveries in Otley. Guyson

International of North Avenue announced million-dollar expansion. Paul Madeley store in Market Place closed following inclusion in £27m take-over deal by Ward White.

1988: Go ahead given for new £225,000 day hospital to be built. Tributes flooded in to Wharfe Valley Times following tragic death of Chief Reporter, Dawn Cawood (26). Deer antler found on possible site of Neolithic settlement near banks of River Wharfe. Old 'hot metal' system for printing 'Wharfedale & Airedale Observer' and 'The Ilkley Gazette' was replaced by new technology. Solicitor, J Colin Greenwood of Barret Chamberlain, retired after 40 years. Vaults discovered under former stable at Whitakers Arms, Kirkgate. 100 years since Otley St John Ambulance Brigade held first meeting. New Inn, Market Place, closed for last time and windows boarded up. Walter Hamby sold Red Lion to Smiths Tadcaster Breweries Ltd. Work started on Otley's new shopping development 'New Inn Court.' Mrs Kathleen Innes retired as Secretary of Otley Show after 33 years. Former 'Presto' store in Boroughgate re-opened as 'In Shops' comprising 43 shop units. Maternity Unit at Otley Hospital closed despite campaigns to keep it open. Mr John W Greetham, former partner in Atkinson Dacre & Slack, Solicitors, died aged 46 years. Mr Leslie Hill of Lofthouse, Hill & Harrison retired from veterinary practice after 43 years. Teale & Son, bakers and confectioners, celebrated 50th anniversary.

1989: Progress is being made on Orchardgate development. Discovered that Otley Parish Church might date back to Anglo Saxon times. Gavin Brown (23) of Willeton District CC, Australia joined Otley Town Cricket Club. Don Estelle, singing star of television's 'It aint half hot, Mum' visited the 'In Shops.' £5m was spent on Otley Hospital. Woolworths marked 50 years of trading in Otley. Town set for Sunday shopping. Airport flying time extended by 1 hour. Otley Little Theatre opened Golden Jubilee season. All divisions of Ogden Group of Companies left Otley for new premises. Otley Social Working Mens Club had 25th Anniversary. Parish Church Rainbow Unit formed. After 60 years, Otley Royal British Legion Women's Section closed due to lack of members.

HRH Princess of Wales greatly welcomed at Spring Gardens Residential Home.

1990: Otley became Ireland when YTV brought cameras to film 'The Ireland Project.' Otley Bus Depot closed. Car parking charges introduced on town centre car parks. Over 90 mph gusts of wind left trail of damage. Teal Beck Flats complex 'topped out' by TV personality Richard Whiteley. 100% pass rate for Otley Rhythmic Gymnastics in National Development Grading. First Otley River Festival. Free car park opened near Cross Pipes public house in Westgate. National Condom Week highlighted risk of AIDS. Francis Verity of F W Verity, Opticians, retired after more than 50 years. Work started on new Parish Church meeting room. 26 October editions of 'Wharfedale & Airedale Observer' and 'Ilkley Gazette, were first issues printed at Hall Ings, Bradford. M A Shaw, jewellers, closed after 80 years of association with Otley. Norman Jackson (Sooty) chimneysweep retired after 40 years.

1991: Locals prayed for peace as Gulf War loomed. Netto grocery store opened opposite bus station. Gypsies left site in Riverdale Road in disgusting state. Boys from Prince Henry's Grammar School found mortar bombs near River Wharfe. Michael Sinclair of Wm Sinclair & Sons Ltd retired. New Parish Church meeting room opened. Refurbishment work at Otley Methodist Church, including new ceiling and windows, was completed. Former Wesleyan Methodist Church in Boroughgate was converted into flats. Kwik-Fit opened on former Bus Depot site. Dr Metcalfe retired from Bridge Street practice after 36 years in Otley. Silver Jubilee of Stephen H Smith Garden & Leisure Centre in Otley. Burglars escaped with safe and substantial amount of money from Leeds Permanent Building Society, Market Place. Town officials given 'key' to Gallows Hill which had been given a face lift. Joe Johnson, snooker player, was rushed to Otley Wharfedale General Hospital following collapse at health club. Otley is 'best blooming town in the whole of Yorkshire and Humberside.' Italy played against United States in World Cup at Otley's Cross Green Ground and won 30 - 9. Methodist Church sold crockery to raise church funds. Motorcyclist enthusiasts from past shared reminiscences at first reunion at Korks held by former British Sand Racing Champion Richard Agar. Princess Royal visited Acrecliffe Riding School in Otley. Sidney Cooper (93) first to move into Chevin Court Retirement Homes in Boroughgate.

1992 - Joyce Butler's house converted to 1960s look for use in 'Heartbeat.' Wharfedale General Hospital got keyhole surgery by partly donated Special Equipment Fund monies. Damage to Otley's War Memorial in Garden of Remembrance was accidental and second in eleven years. Residents in Throstle Nest Close, Riverside Park Estate, St Davids Road and Carr Bank won boundary battle to stay under control of North Yorkshire Council and not move into control of Leeds City Council. Tonia Hearne became live model for a day in window of Imperial Cancer Research Shop. Fleece Hotel had a team comprising of David Cottam, Mick Barton and Dave Wellbourn in YTV's programme 'Time Please.' Breast Diagnostic Unit was up and running at Wharfedale General Hospital only 15 months after launch of £200,000 Early Bird Appeal. New ramp at Post Office gave access for the disabled. Oxfam held Fashion Show at Civic Centre. Otley Retired Men's Forum reached 21st Anniversary. Mystery closure of gym in Westgate Arcade left many members out of pocket. Otley Methodist Church Choir disbanded after 50 years due to shortage of choirmaster and young people. Dawn Acton, Tracy Barlow of Coronation Street, opened showbiz shop in 'In Shops.' Bitumen between stone setts in Market Place melted with summertime heat and got trampled into shops. Gas Showroom on Kirkgate closed but tobacconist, James Barber, stepped in and became official British Gas Agent, enabling local residents to settle accounts and obtain tokens and energy stamps. First Folk Festival attracted more than 1,500 folk fans. Produmax landed with £648,000 contract. Wartime bombs found in Leslie Chew's lock-up garage in Ash Grove. Norman Graville became first person in Wharfedale to be awarded a Certificate of Merit by Yorkshire Beekeepers' Association.

1993: New crossing in Billams Hill was officially opened. Dr. John Arrand, formerly of Otley, created world's first cancer vaccine drug. P Garnett & Sons Ltd announced 250 new jobs due to expansion. Businesses who lost trade following roadworks in Westgate last year were refused compensation from Leeds City Council. Betting Shop in Market Place given go-ahead despite protests. Otley Chamber of Trade changed its name to Otley Chamber of Trade and Commerce. Orchardgate units became available to lease from £100 per week. Otley Rugby Club won Courage League title and two county trophies in space of four days. Crazy Golf Course officially opened in Wharfemeadows Park by Christopher Chittell (Eric Pollard of Emmerdale). May Day traditions were revived by Otley's Buttercross Belles. Leeds City Council decided not to re-open Wharfemeadows Swimming Pool. Otley Choral Society celebrated 50th Anniversary. Sundial in Wharfemeadows Park in memory of Sam Hartley Chippendale was officially unveiled by his children. Otley Handbell Ringers were presented with 150-year-old set of tubular bells from Mrs Jessie Graham which formerly belonged to her grandfather, John Nelson, plumber in Courthouse Street. Hundreds attended health march against hospital closure. Roman road discovered on edge of town at Ellar Ghyll. Cheque for £50,000 handed over to Otley Rugby Union Football Club for Youth development. Otley Rotary Club celebrated its Diamond Jubilee Year with a dinner for 90 members and guests at Otley Golf Club.

1994: Solicitor, Mercia Cato, retired from Newstead & Walker after 31 years. A Milner Bank house was in gas explosion and attended by Otley and Rawdon fire-fighters. Post Office announced its intention to change Nelson Street from a Crown Office to Agency status. Otley Rotary Club made history when it introduced its first lady members. Parents voted to keep Prince Henry's Grammar School under Leeds Education Authority and not to make it of a grant maintained status. Closure of Westgate due to road works caused chaos. Job Lot, In Shops, opened by Reg Holdsworth of Coronation Street. Annie Nicholson honoured for 60 years' service to Royal British Legion. TV programme '999' re-lived moorland rescue of Liz Brooke after fall from horse. Former Otley Drama Teacher, Bea Kelly, had part in 'Crimewatch.' Water geyser in Ilkley Road sent sand flying. Visitors flocked to David Asquith's go-karting track in Pool Road over Bank Holiday. Eric Shaw, one of the founders of Weston Lane Junior Sports & Social Club, died aged 67 in New Zealand. Otley fish fryer, Ady Atter, raised £20,000 in walk from John O' Groates to Lands End. Actress Jenny Agutter and director Kay Mellor, were in

Otley to film a movie 'Sweet Surrender.' Actor Dennis Waterman filmed part of new series 'Circle of Deceipt' on Otley Chevin. Post Office took over gas payments from James R Barber following Post Office Counters' negotiations with British Gas. District goes lottery crazy and Safeway, Woolworths & Wharfe View News were appointed ticket sellers. 'Strange but True' filmed at Bridge Street Surgery included Lorraine Ham, faith healer. New hall at Congregational Church re-opened following fire. Police Station now closed to public at night.

1995: Centenary of Ted Smith & Son, Bondgate. Raging bullock ran riot in town before going for swim in river. Yorkshire Electricity in Orchard Gate closed. Dacre Son & Hartley celebrated 175 years in business in Otley. Otley Mills' 100 feet chimney saved from demolition with thanks to essential repair work. Chippendale Junior School changed its name to Thomas Chippendale Primary School. 24-hour flying introduced at Leeds Bradford Airport. Otley's Saturday market to have stalls on Kirkgate. First electric passenger trains ran on Wharfedale line between Ilkley and Leeds. Newall Infant School closed its doors after 58 years. VJ beacon lit on Chevin to mark 50 years of peace. Internet arrived at Prince Henry's Grammar School via Bradford University. Wharfedale Newspapers moved into Orchardgate. Yorkshire Water laid Cable TV pipes along with own on Otley Bridge. Norman Wilkinson to replace Michael Rhodes as Chairman of Otley Bench in new year. Citizens Advice Bureau opened in Courthouse Street following move from Civic Centre. Dialling codes changed again.

1996: First day of 1996 saw County Court doors closed for last time after more than 100 years. Former Wharfemeadows swimming pool re-opened as Leisure Complex. Civic Centre became more wheelchair friendly. Argos opened new store in Boroughgate. Community play 'A Heart Shaped Field' was a sell-out. Quarrying at Bridge End came to an end after more than 50 years. Stephen H Smith opened new extension and celebrated 30 years of trading. 200th anniversary of Otley Show. Loyalty Card was launched offering special discounts to Otley shoppers. First Otley Vintage Transport Extravaganza organised by Nigel Francis. Wharfe Valley Times moved to Market Street. Announcement made that Otley would be unlikely to receive TV Channel 5 when broadcasting started. Dr James Richmond, general practitioner, retired from Otley Bridge Street practice.

1997: Traders concerned about number of Charity Shops in Otley. Yellow boxes planned for Crossgate/Boroughgate and Burras Lane/Kirkgate junctions. Armed robbers burst into Midland Bank and made off with cash. Rev David Woodward of The Methodist Church went on European Pilgrimage. Stunning picture of the Comet Hale-Bopp was taken by Martin Middlemiss, Butcher. Otley Magistrates Court closed for final time. Long-awaited pedestrian traffic lights in Manor Square were turned on and branded a danger to pedestrians. Bingo Hall closed due to loss of £500 per week. Prince Henry's Grammar School pupils, Matthew and Andrew Maidens, died in car accident. TV Presenters, Claire Frisby and Mike McCarthy, opened new PDSA shop in Kirkgate.

Garnetts Mill got £2.5m boost with new equipment. Bay Horse in Market Place was given gold award for best public house in Leeds District. Otley was like a ghost town whilst people watched televised funeral of Diana, Princess of Wales. Conversion of former Church Hall, Burras Lane into houses commenced. Mr Ray Jenkinson of Wrenbeck Drive suggested cable car idea for Otley Chevin to mark the Millennium. Empty double decker bus rolled out of control across busy road narrowly missing pedestrian and crashed into Netto.

1998: Middlemiss & Son, family butchers, named in new BBC's Good Food Guide 'The Best of British Beef and where to buy it.' Oxfam in Westgate closed after 30 years. Craftsman Tools won award and £120,000 grant from Department of Trade & Industry sponsored by Smart Awards. Needle and thread in a colourful embroidered panel captured Town's history. It had taken Otley Townswomen Guild nine years to complete. The Shoppers' Loyalty card introduced in September 1996 had run its course and was scrapped. Visitors to Wharfedale General Hospital faced car-parking charges of 50p for the first 2 hours and then 50p for each successive hour. Staff were already paying £5 per month for parking discs. Second bank robbery at Midland Bank within 14 months. Business dismay as 12th charity shop moved into town. £84,000 repair project started on Otley Parish Church. Pharmacist Roger Whitworth retired after almost 29 years at Mainprize & Wood, Kirkgate. Coronation Street's 'Fred Elliott' officially opened newly refurbished 'Weegmann' shop. Gym Owner, James Jiora of World Class Sports & Fitness in Boroughgate, landed big contract in Nigeria. Shopmobility, a scooter scheme to help the elderly and disabled, was launched at Otley Civic Centre.

1999: Skate Park opened in Wharfemeadows Park following fund raising by 'Space to Grow' group and TV programme 'Action time'. YTV weather girl, Debbie Lindley, came to Rowleys Hairdressers to look at innovative hairstyles. Chevin cross came down on Surprise View for last time in its present form. Plans under way to construct a stronger but lighter one made out of wood for next year. Ghostly goings-on at the British Heart Foundation Shop on Kirkgate/Market Place frightened shop staff. Otley residents up in arms over huge 'Welcome to Leeds' signs which had gone up at all town entrances. Otley won £30,000 lottery money to build millenium green. Town urged to use television fame for trade. Refugees from war torn Kosovo flew into Leeds Bradford Airport. Otley first choice as site of new hospital. 'Wheelie' bins invaded most homes in Otley and Guiseley. 2,000 local people watched eclipse from top of Chevin despite its being marred by clouds. Fight was on to save former Wharfe Street School. Sainsburys wanted town centre store and vowed to create 150 jobs. Former newsreader Angela Rippon drove a yellow Morgan from Otley Classic Car Hire Company in BBC television holiday programme. Wharfedale & Airedale Observer voters said no to Sainsbury Store. Bulldozers flattened former Beech Hill Cinema/Bingo Hall. Altrix Healthcare of Otley was behind UK's first major breakthrough in drug and alcohol testing for more than 20 years. Former headmaster of North Parade Secondary School, Mr Harry M Spenceley, died aged 95 years. Around 70 people turned out to heave new Millenium Easter Cross into place at Surprise View on the Chevin, which had been made from timber salvaged from the 1996 IRA Manchester bombing. Local services were ready for the Millenium Bug which never happened.

2000: Bus service from Otley to Menston Railway Station launched. After 65 years, the last Auction was held at Bridge End Auction Mart in February before its closure. Transco dismantled 100-year-old redundant gasholder just off Gay Lane. John Bird, partner in Newstead & Walker, retired after 40 years. Otley Civic Centre fitted with automatic doors costing £10,000. Ashfield House, a Grade II listed building, went on the market. The garden of Yvette & Jim Wilks of Bridge Street was given a makeover by BBC TV's 'Garden Invaders.' Dr Geoffrey Hall of Bridge Street Surgery left for Spain. Magistrate, David Tempest (51) lost his fight to live following local road accident. Fury at closure of Otley Tourist Information centre. Millenium green plan for land at Otley Mills donated by Ronnie Duncan was scuppered by pollution. Enthusiasts waved farewell to Concorde as it left Leeds Bradford Airport in June for the last time. Oasis star, Liam Gallagher, made surprise visit to Jon's Menswear and bought a T-shirt. Tributes were paid at the funeral of Mr C Norman Hindle, one of Otley's characters, who died aged 83 years. Otley Methodist Church launched £100,000 appeal for refurbishment. Market traders grudgingly bent to Europe regulations and switched to metric weight. Fist fights and panic food buying marked start of petrol crisis through refinery blockades and go-slow traffic protests. Yorkshire MEP, David Bowe, officially opened new Language College at Prince Henry's Grammar School. Lift off for first Air Ambulance from Airport. Otley Rugby Union Club lined up against Leicester Tigers for biggest ever match and lost to Leicester 11 to 83. Sir Jimmy Savile officially opened James Barber's new cigar lounge. Robinson Crusoe panto, by Otley Little Theatre, still went ahead despite theft of several costumes. 15 homes in Piper Lane/Westgate area were flooded with filthy water and sewage only weeks before Christmas.

2001: New Otley Hospital given go-ahead on present Newall site and should be completed by 2004. Chippendale Room in Civic Centre was officially opened by Town Mayor, Cllr Christine Campbell. The Hymers family of Otley appeared in Channel 4's programme 'The 1940's House.' Foot and mouth outbreak began to affect local farmers and temporarily closed Wharfedale Farmers Auction Mart in Leeds Road. Otley Show cancelled due to foot and mouth outbreak costing organisers the sum of £20,000. Pensioner, Lila Mitchell, handed over holiday money to Otley Lions Indian Earthquake Appeal. Sainsburys pulled out of plans to build supermarket in town. Otley Action for Older People scooped around £182,000 from The National Lottery Charities Board. Footh and mouth crisis forced Carnival organisers to cancel. Campaigners won fight against housing development between Meagill Rise and St Davids Road. Town received £1m from Government to help it get back on its feet following foot and mouth crisis. Protests failed to save Thomas Chippendale and All Saints Junior Schools from closure. A play called 'The Hard Road' was held in marquee at Our Lady & All Saints Church. It told the story of how the Irish came to Otley. Dancing teacher, Carol Newbould, who runs the Newall School of Dancing, celebrated 40 years of teaching. Royal Engineer, Matthew Simpson, was amongst first to go to Macedonia during conflict. Samuel

Curzon was nominated for prestigious award after tackling robbers at Safeway Supermarket. Four apartments in newly converted former Liberal Club went up for sale, prices ranging from £120,000 to £152,500. Emmerdale actor, John Middleton (aka Ashley the Vicar) re-opened newly refurbished Oxfam shop. Thanks to Otley Disability Advisory Group, a ramp was installed at Gallows Hill Nature Reserve for the disabled. BBC 'Look North' presenter, Harry Gration, dropped in to Safeway to promote the Victorian Fayre. Chris Boardman and his family growled down the telephone and won £1,000 in Kellogg's 'Grrowl for a Grrrand Competition. A scaled model and artist's impression of proposed new Wharfedale General Hospital went on display at Civic Centre for two days. Otley Karate Centre picked up no less than 28 trophies, including six England titles, at Shukokai Karate Union 2001 National Championships in Manchester. Stone memorial was unveiled at Our Lady & All Saints Church in memory of potato famine victims. Wharfedale FM Radio went on air for nine days between 7.00 a.m. and 11.00 p.m.

2002: A ginnel which runs from Boroughgate to Courthouse Street could now be added to town's official footpaths. A Harry Potter reading marathon raised £5,680 for breast cancer relief. Work began on £345,000 project to modernise Otley Indoor Swimming Baths. Threshers off-licence in Kirkgate was ram-raided. In February, the River Wharfe burst its banks, resulting in closure of bridge to traffic. Otley Town's pitches suffered as result of bad weather and games had to be postponed.

Below: An unusual view of Otley Bridge and Wharfemeadows Park taken from the Chevin around 1995.

1952 – 2002 National Milestones

1952: Death of King George VI.

1953: Coronation of HRH Queen Elizabeth II.

1954: Food rationing ended. ITV started.

1955: Churchill resigned. Suez. Hungarian uprising.

1956: Premium Bonds introduced. First Campaign for Nuclear Disarmament march from Aldermaston.

1957: Britain's first hydrogen bomb exploded. Derek Ibbotson world mile record.

1958: M1 opened. Hovercraft demonstrated.

1960: Farthing scrapped. Princess Margaret married Antony Armstrong-Jones.

1961: South Africa left Commonwealth. Tristan da Cunha volcano erupted.

1962: Attempted assassination of De Gaulle. Missiles in Cuba. Telstar in sky. First James Bond film 'Dr. No'.

1963: John F Kennedy assassinated. Nuclear test ban treaty. Olympic ideal ruined by politics. Beatles achieved international fame.

1964: BBC2 launched. Tokyo Olympics. Golds for Rand, Packer, Davies and Matthews.

1965: Death penalty abolished. Churchill died. Rhodesia declared UDI.

1966: England won World Cup.

1967: Colour TV. De Gaulle said 'Non'. Breath tests. QE2 launched by Queen Elizabeth II. Dr. Christian Barnard transplanted heart.

1968: Race relations Bill. No more steam on British Rail.

1969: First man on the moon. First troops in Northern Ireland.

1970: Equal Pay Act. Divorce permitted in Italy.

1971: Decimal currency.

1972: The Queen's Silver Wedding Anniversary.

1973: Britain entered EEC. Princess Anne married Captain Mark Phillips.

1972: USA's Mark Spitz won seven Olympic Golds.

1974: Flixborough tragedy.

1975: Headingley Test wicket vandalised.

1976: Margaret Thatcher became Tory Leader. Harold Wilson resigned. Olympic ideal ruined by politics. General Franco and Field Marshall Viscount Montgomery died.

1977: Joe Haines hits headlines. Jimmy Carter made it to the White House.

1979: Margaret Thatcher appointed Prime Minister. Russia invaded Afghanistan.

1980: Polish shipyard strike led by Lech Walesa. John Lennon assassinated.

1981: Ronald Reagan inaugurated 40th President of USA. Prince Charles and Lady Diana Spencer married. US launched first space shuttle. Francois Mitterrand elected French President.

1982: Argentina seized the Falkland Islands.

1984: First untethered space walk. Miner's strike led by 'King Arthur' Scargill. Golden Temple at Amritsar attack. Prime Minister Indira Gandhi assassinated.

1985: Bob Geldof Live Aid concert.

1986: Chernobyl Nuclear explosion in Russia. Argentina won World Cup in Mexico. US planes bombed Libya. Soviet Space Station MIR launched. Prince Andrew and Sarah Ferguson married.

1988: Gorbachev elected President of Russia. George Bush elected President of U.S.A.

1989: Berlin Wall broken down.

1990: Reunification of Germany. Poll tax riots led to resignation of Margaret Thatcher as prime minister. Hubble Space Telescope launched. Iraq invaded Kuwait.

1991 Freddie Mercury died of AIDS.

1992: Bill Clinton elected US President. Bosnia claimed independence in Yugoslavia. Serbs revolted with ethnic cleansing. Yugoslav Civil War. Princess Anne divorced and married Captain Timothy Laurence, RN.

1993: World Health Organisation reported 47 million infected with AIDS.

1994: Rwandan Civil War. Channel tunnel opened. Nelson Mandela elected State President of South Africa.

1997: Tony Blair became Prime Minister. Information released on Dolly the cloned sheep. China reclaimed Hong Kong. Diana, Princess of Wales, killed in a car accident.

1998: France won the World Cup. Anglo-American bombinf of Iraq.

1999: Prince Edward married Sophie Rhys-Jones.

2000: Milosevic fell from power.

2002: Princess Margaret died aged 71 years. Queen Mother died aged 101 years.

Through all this Her Majesty the Queen reigned glorious and victorious.

Martin Bentley Baton

Martin Bentley is the current holder of Otley Sports Council's 'Jack Simpson Award for Achievement in Sport'. This was gained following his success in the Special Olympics, a competition devoted to those with a disability. Otley Sports Council has successfully nominated him to be part of the

relay team carrying the Queen's baton around the Commonwealth leading up to the official opening of the Commonwealth games in Manchester in 2002.

Well done, Martin.

And we also say well done to Vernon Marston at The Bay Horse for his contribution to Britain in Bloom and funds raised for The Marie Curie Foundation as a result of his efforts.

Glimpse of the Future

Otley's New Maypole

A project to erect a new 20 foot maypole, put forward by Wayzgoose and the Buttercross Belles and supported by Town Council and Local Heritage grants, is expected to be com-

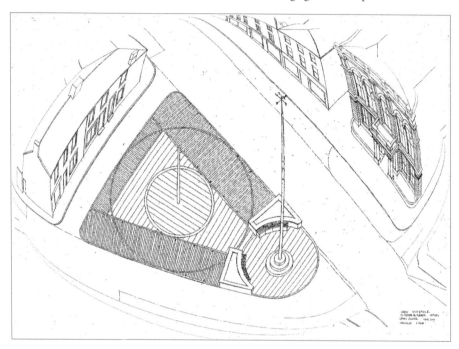

pleted by the autumn of 2002. The Cross Green site will be restored to its original purpose, thus reclaiming some of Otley's heritage. The car park opposite the Civic Centre will be re-laid with block paving and York stone to provide a suitable dancing surface.

The new maypole will be in the centre of the area and the flagpole will remain in its existing position. It is intended that the square will still be used for car parking when not being used for other purposes.

When we looked back over the past 25 years to see what had happened in our town, we realised what almost unbelievable changes had taken place in the world.

Who would have thought that Concorde would come to Yeadon? That we'd travel to Montereau under the Channel, not over it! That there would be tourists in space, Dolly the Sheep, computers for all, CDs, DVDs, satellite communications and navigation including mobile phones. We hadn't imagined DNA testing, AIDS, micro surgery and non-invasive surgery, BSE, bungy jumping, traffic gridlocks, the return of trams, the cost of petrol at 80p a litre - and litres, not gallons. Theme parks, global warming, fleece clothing, National Lottery, Post-its, animal passports, digi-cams, playstations, Iraq, plc building societies and the trials and tribulations of the Royal Family.

So what of Otley in the future. Could we see trains again? A new hospital (perhaps with more than the present hospitals one sloping corridor as shown in our picture?), a sports or an arts centre, regional government perhaps, with boundary changes? Or a footbridge for Burley and maybe a second bridge in Otley? Electric cars, a helicopter transport link, even a bypass? Maybe another annual event to add to our calendar? Even some brave soul to update this in another twenty five years and a new library to keep it in! One exciting development is the first local Farmer's Market to be held in Otley, just a few days before this Queen's Jubilee. We wish it every success.

One national trend that has impacted on Otley is an increasingly litigious society, resulting in more and more health and safety legislation which makes it difficult for anyone to take responsibility for others on a voluntary, or even statutory, basis.

Whatever happens, we are sure that people will continue to enjoy our lovely market town in its beautiful setting. We hope this book has given you some pleasure and posed a few questions.

Thank you again for supporting Otley.

Thomas Chippendale

With deep imprint in history's pages
Your name is set in lines of gold;
A torch will light that page extolling
That craft so treasured and so old.

This market town that you so honoured
With craftmanship so rich and rare,
Applauds your name so steeped in greatness
Of beauty carved beyond compare.

God's tree was turned to sculptured beauty
A living tribute to your name,
Emblazoned on the world forever
You brought us honour, pride and fame.

2002

Lila Mitchell
(Now in her nineties)